Why You Need An Expo... Hebrews 1-4

Steven J. Cole

Why You Need Jesus Christ:
An Exposition of Hebrews 1-4

© Steven J. Cole, 2024, All Rights Reserved

First Published: July 2024

Unless otherwise identified, Scripture quotations are from *The New American Standard Bible* (NASB), © The Lockman Foundation 1960, 1962, 1963, 1968, 1971, 1972, 1973, 1975, 1977, and 1995.

Books by Steven J. Cole: *Riches from the Word* Series (practical expositions of biblical texts) available on Amazon.com:

- *Philippians: Enduring Joy*
- *James: Activate: Do the Word*
- *Haggai, Zechariah, & Malachi: God's Light for Dark Times*
- *Ezra & Nehemiah: Spiritual Renewal and Rebuilding*
- *Knowing that You Know Christ: 1, 2, & 3 John*
- *Laying Hold of God: Old Testament Lessons on Prayer*
- *The Christian Home: A Refuge of Love*
- *Lessons for God's Servants: The Life of Moses (1)*
- *Lessons on Life and Leadership: The Life of Moses (2)*
- *Growing Solid Through Suffering: 1 Peter*
- *Foundation for Spiritual Growth: 2 Peter*
- *You're Rich—in Christ: An Exposition of Ephesians 1-3*
- *Walking Worthily: An Exposition of Ephesians 4:1-5:20*
- *The Family and the Fight: An Exposition of Ephesians 5:21-6:24*
- *God's Solution for Sin: An Exposition of Romans 1-5*
- *God's Strategy for Holiness. An Exposition of Romans 6-8*
- *God's Sovereign Grace: An Exposition of Romans 9-11*
- *The Service of the Saints: An Exposition of Romans 12-16*
- *The Best News in the World: 23 Christmas Sermons*
- *When I Find Time: New Year's and Other Sermons on Time*

Obedience—or Not? Expository Lessons on the Kings of Judah
Snapshots of Faith: An Exposition of Hebrews 11 & Judges 6-8
The Supremacy of Jesus Christ: An Exposition of Colossians
Conduct in the Household of God: An Exposition of 1 Timothy
Healthy Doctrine: An Exposition of 2 Timothy
Zealous for Good Works: An Exposition of Titus & Philemon
The Coming of Our Lord Jesus: An Exposition of 1 Thessalonians
Instructions for the End Times: An Exposition of 2 Thessalonians
Improving Your Witness

Also by Steven J. Cole:
Great Christians You Should Know: What I've Learned from Reading Christian Biographies
The Basics of the Christian Life: The A, B, Cs for Christian Growth
Why You Need the Church (Even With Its Problems)

Table of Contents

Foreword 5
~1~ God has Spoken (Hebrews 1:1-2a) 7
~2~ The Supremacy of the Son (Hebrews 1:2b-3) 19
~3~ The Son's Supremacy Over Angels (Hebrews 1:4-14) 29
~4~ The Danger of Drifting Spiritually (Hebrews 2:1-4) 41
~5~ Our Glorious Destiny in Christ (Hebrews 2:5-9) 51
~6~ Why Jesus' Death Was Fitting (Hebrews 2:10) 61
~7~ Jesus Our Brother and Savior (Hebrews 2:11-15) 71
~8~ Why Jesus Became a Man (Hebrews 2:16-18) 81
~9~ To Endure, Consider Jesus (Hebrews 3:1-6) 91
~10~ A Warning Against Hardness of Heart (Hebrews 3:7-11) 101
~11~ Persevering in Faith (Hebrews 3:12-19) 111
~12~ Cultural Religion Versus Saving Faith (Hebrews 4:1-11) 121
~13~ God's Powerful Word (Hebrews 4:12-13) 131
~14~ The Throne of Grace (Hebrews 4:14-16) 141

Foreword

We live in a time when many who formerly professed faith in Christ are "deconstructing" their faith. They think that following Christ was too costly, or it didn't deliver what they had hoped for. They prayed, but God didn't deliver them from some difficult trials. Some get sucked into the pleasures of the world. Or, perhaps they got burned by other professing Christians and conclude that if Christianity was real, Christians wouldn't act like that. Some get lured into sexual sins or the LGBTQ+ movement. There are probably dozens more reasons that people do not persevere in their faith.

But this is not a recent problem. In the first century, some Jewish believers in Jesus were going through persecution and difficult trials. They were tempted to abandon Jesus and go back into Judaism, which was more culturally accepted than the newer Christian faith was. They needed endurance (Heb. 10:36). The key to such endurance was (and still is) to look to Jesus Christ, who for the joy set before Him endured the cross (Heb. 12:2-3).

In Hebrews 1-4, the author points to Jesus as the supreme person in all human history. He is superior to the prophets (1:1-3); to the angels (1:4-2:18); to Moses (3:1-19); and, to Joshua (4:1-16). Thus we can trust Him and draw near to Him for help in every trial that we encounter. In the next volume (forthcoming, on Hebrews 5-10), we will see that Jesus is the supreme priest through whom we can approach God's holy presence. I have already completed the volume on Hebrews 11, *Snapshots of Faith*, where the author gives examples of those who have endured great trials through faith in the Lord. A final future volume will cover Hebrews 12-13 on enduring faith.

This volume is edited from sermons that I preached at Flagstaff Christian Fellowship, Flagstaff, Arizona, from November 2003 through March 2004. The original manuscripts and audio messages can currently be accessed on Bible.org, fcfonline.org, and Precept-Austin.org. I pray that the Lord will use this volume to magnify our glorious Savior and show why you need Him to endure whatever trials you may be facing.

Steven J. Cole
Flagstaff, Arizona, July 2024

Hebrews 1:1-2a, New American Standard Bible 1995

1 God, after He spoke long ago to the fathers in the prophets in many portions and in many ways, 2 in these last days has spoken to us in His Son, ...

God Has Spoken
Hebrews 1:1-2a

All of the world's religions and philosophies attempt to answer the fundamental questions of our frail and short human lives: Is there a God? Can we know Him? If so, how? How can we make sense of the trials of this life and the certainty of death? Does it really matter what you believe, as long as you're sincere?

The Letter to the Hebrews answers all of these basic questions. But I will warn you, its answers cut cross-grain to the popular views of our day. We live in a time when being tolerant and non-judgmental are primary virtues. Truth is viewed as subjective and personal, not absolute and universal. Thus, if Buddhism makes sense to you and gives you fulfillment, who am I to say that you are wrong? If you believe in Islam, Hinduism, Judaism, or any other of the world's religions (or any combination of them), as long as you're not hurting others, it would be judgmental of me to say that you are believing a lie. That is the prevailing mindset of our tolerant culture. The only person they will not tolerate is someone who insists that his view is the *only* true view.

The Letter to the Hebrews cuts across this modern mindset by affirming that God is, that He has spoken, and that His Son, who is the epitome of His revelation, is supreme over all. He demands total allegiance. He is not tolerant of any rivals. To turn away from Him to any other system or way of approaching God is to turn toward certain judgment. He alone will help us make sense of our trials. Thus we must consider Him more fully, submit to Him at all times, and trust Him in all the trials of life.

So the **theme** of Hebrews is that ***the absolute supremacy of Jesus Christ should motivate us to enduring faith in the face of trials.*** While almost all scholars agree with that theme, there are many divergent opinions on some of the background matters of this letter.

As you probably know, there is a debate over **who wrote Hebrews**. Many say that the apostle Paul wrote it (perhaps A. W. Pink is the most convincing on this position). The earliest statement on the author is from Clement of Alexandria (c.155-c.220), who said that Paul wrote it in Hebrew and that Luke translated it into Greek (quoted in Eusebius, *Ecclesiastical History*, 6.14.2, A.D.

325). But the language and thought forms are not like those of Paul. And, the statement in 2:3-4 seems to indicate that the author, like his readers, was a second-generation Christian who had believed the testimony of the apostles. But Paul heard the gospel directly from the risen Lord Jesus Christ (Gal. 1:12-17).

If Paul did not write Hebrews, who did? Other suggestions have included Barnabas (Tertullian, c. 225, is the earliest proponent), Apollos (Luther's view), and Priscilla (Harnack). All of the views have problems, and so we probably should conclude, with the early church father, Origen (died c. 254), that "God only knows the truth" about who wrote Hebrews.

Perhaps because of the lack of agreement about authorship, there is also a divergence of opinion about **the date** Hebrews was written and **the place** to which it was written. Clement of Rome seems to quote it in about A.D. 96. Most scholars agree that it had to be written before the destruction of the temple in Jerusalem in A.D. 70. If this cataclysmic event had happened, it would have contributed to the author's argument about the supremacy of Christianity over Judaism, but there is no mention of this.

The recipients of the letter were suffering persecution, but not yet to the point of martyrdom (10:32-34; 12:4). This last fact seems to rule out the church in Jerusalem as the recipients of the letter, since both Stephen and James had been martyred there early on. At the conclusion of the letter (13:24), the author sends greetings from "those from Italy." This could mean those living in Italy, where the writer is also living, or those from Italy who are living away and sending their greetings back home. If the latter is the case, the letter was probably written to Christians in Rome just before the outbreak of the persecution under Nero in A.D. 64. But we must remain tentative in these matters.

To whom was Hebrews written? The title of the book "goes back to the last quarter of the second century, if not earlier" (F. F. Bruce, *Commentary on the Epistle to the Hebrews* [Eerdmans], p. xxiii), but was not a part of the original manuscript. Most scholars agree that it was written to a group of second-generation Jewish believers in Jesus Christ, who were tempted because of persecution to go back to Judaism. It is filled with Old Testament quotes and allusions, and it presupposes a detailed knowledge of the Jewish sacrificial system.

These people had begun well, submitting joyfully to trials and persecution (10:32-34). But as the trials continued, some of them were stalled in their Christian growth. They were thinking back to the good old days, when they could go through the motions of their Jewish religion without much interference. (Judaism was a tolerated religion in the Roman Empire, but Christianity was not.) Their foreboding about the looming persecution tempted them to abandon their faith in Christ and go back to Judaism. They were tempted to opt for temporary relief, but at the expense of abandoning the supremacy and uniqueness of Jesus Christ.

So the author writes, very strongly at times, to warn the readers against this danger. He refers to his letter as "a word of exhortation" (13:22). It contains several strong warning sections (2:1-3; 3:12-19; 6:4-8; 10:26-31; 12:25-29). We all are prone to drift into our former ways of life, especially when it is difficult and costly to follow Jesus. Also, second generation believers are often more prone to fall into an outward, go-through-the-motions kind of religion, as opposed to a vital, personal relationship with Jesus Christ. Hebrews exposes the inadequacy of that kind of formal religion and shows that we must have an enduring faith in the person and work of Jesus Christ.

Hebrews is the only New Testament document that expressly calls Jesus a priest, although it is implied in others (Bruce, p. lii). It shows how Jesus fulfilled the entire Old Testament ceremonial system of the temple and sacrifices. Perhaps the Book of Hebrews is the closest thing we have to an inspired expansion of what Jesus must have told the two men on the Emmaus Road (Luke 24:27): "Then beginning with Moses and with all the prophets, He explained to them the things concerning Himself in all the Scriptures."

Gleason Archer observed (*The Epistle to the Hebrews* [Baker], p. 4),

The Church must ever revert to this sublime Epistle in order to bring the two Testaments into focus with each other. More than any other single book, *Hebrews* serves to demonstrate the underlying unity of the sixty-six books of the Bible as proceeding ultimately from one and the same divine author, the blessed Holy Spirit.

The author of Hebrews has an unusual way of citing Old Testament scriptures, in that he almost always neglects the human author and instead ascribes the quotes to God (Leon Morris, *Expositor's Bible Commentary*, ed. by Frank Gaebelein [Zondervan], 12:7). (See, for example, 1:5, 6, 7, 13; 2:11-12; 10:5 [ascribed to Christ]; 3:7; 10:15 [ascribed to the Holy Spirit].) As Leon Morris (*ibid.*) puts it, "The effect is to emphasize the divine authorship of the whole OT. For the author, what Scripture says, God says."

Again, the overall theme is that because Jesus Christ is supreme over all, Christians must endure their current trials by faith. A brief outline of the book is:

1. Jesus Christ is superior to all in His person (1:1-4:16).
   A. Jesus Christ is superior to the prophets (1:1-3).
   B. Jesus Christ is superior to the angels (1:4-2:18).
   C. Jesus Christ is superior to Moses (3:1-19).
   D. Jesus Christ is superior to Joshua (4:1-16).
2. Jesus Christ is superior to all in His priesthood (5:1-10:18).
   A. Jesus Christ is superior to Aaron and his priesthood (5:1-7:28).
   B. Jesus Christ is superior to the Old Covenant (8:1-10:18).
      1) Jesus Christ offers better promises (8:1-13).
      2) Jesus Christ offers a better tabernacle (9:1-14).
      3) Jesus Christ offers a better sacrifice (9:15-10:18).
3. Christ's superiority should stimulate us to enduring faith in the face of trials (10:19-13:25).
   A. Enduring faith obeys God when under trials (10:19-39).
   B. Enduring faith is illustrated throughout the Scriptures (11:1-40).
   C. Enduring faith looks unto Jesus and submits to His discipline (12:1-13).
   D. Enduring faith expresses itself in practical holiness with God's people (12:14-13:25).

With that as an overview and general introduction, let's examine in more detail Hebrews 1:1-2a, which shows that ...

God has spoken to us in His Word, with His Son being the supreme and final revelation.

Hebrews 1:1-2a: "God, after He spoke long ago to the fathers in the prophets in many portions and in many ways, in these last days has spoken to us in His Son, …" The text falls into two sections, God's speaking in the past, and God's speaking in the present.

1. In the past, God spoke to the fathers in the prophets.

The author begins without any formal greetings or comments with two key assumptions: *God is*, and *God has spoken.*

A. God is.

Hebrews 1:1 reminds us of Genesis 1:1, "In the beginning, God …" It doesn't mess around with speculation or philosophizing. It doesn't compile arguments to persuade the skeptic that God exists. It starts with the fact of God. For the author of Hebrews, God is central. He uses the word 68 times, an average of about once every 73 words throughout the book. As Morris says (12:12), "Few NT books speak of God so often."

Someone may say, "But I'm an agnostic; I'm not sure whether or not God exists." Or, "I'm an atheist; I don't believe in God." To all such persons, the Bible says, "Your doubts or your beliefs do not affect the fact that God is." The Bible thrusts God in your face as a prime reality. You ignore Him to your own peril and final destruction. Unbelief is not a matter of rationalism or logic. It is a matter of sin.

B. God has spoken.

He is not silent! He has chosen to reveal Himself to the human race. In Romans 1:18-23, Paul shows how God reveals Himself generally through His creation. People should be able to look at the amazing complexity and design of creation and conclude that there is an awesome Creator. But because people love their sin, they suppress the truth that God reveals through His creation.

The author of Hebrews, writing to Jews who accepted God as the Creator, focuses rather on God's special revelation through the written Word of God. God spoke to the fathers (their Jewish ancestors) in the prophets, a term for all of the Old Testament writers who received and recorded God's message to His people. Thus the author is affirming here what he repeats throughout the book, that the Old Testament was inspired completely by God.

The inspiration of Scripture does not mean that God dictated the very words, although on occasion He did that (*e.g.* the Ten Commandments). Rather, using the different personalities and styles of the various authors, God superintended the process so that the authors recorded without error God's message to us in the words of the original manuscripts. The apostle Peter put it (2 Pet. 1:21), "no prophecy was ever made by an act of human will, but men moved by the Holy Spirit spoke from God." Charles Hodge (*Systematic Theology* [Eerdmans], 1:154) defined inspiration as "an influence of the Holy Spirit on the minds of certain select men, which rendered them the organs of God for the infallible communication of his mind and will. They were in such a sense the organs of God, that what they said God said."

It is important to understand that if God had not chosen to reveal Himself, no one could know Him. Men can speculate and philosophize about what they think God is like, but even the most brilliant discourses on the subject would be mere guesses. Furthermore, the Bible is clear that because of the fall, Satan, "the god of this world has blinded the minds of the unbelieving so that they might not see the light of the gospel of the glory of Christ, who is the image of God" (2 Cor. 4:4). The "natural man does not accept the things of the Spirit of God, for they are foolishness to him; and he cannot understand them, because they are spiritually appraised" (1 Cor. 2:14).

There is a common misconception among evangelicals that anyone can choose at any time to understand the gospel and believe in Jesus Christ. Our job is to explain the gospel, but then people are free to decide whether to believe it or not. But this view seriously underestimates the effects of the fall, and it goes directly against the very words of Jesus. He said (Luke 10:21-22),

> "I praise You, O Father, Lord of heaven and earth, that You have hidden these things from the wise and intelligent and have revealed them to infants. Yes, Father, for this way was well-pleasing in Your sight. All things have been handed over to Me by My Father, and no one knows who the Son is except the Father, and who the Father is except the Son, and anyone to whom the Son wills to reveal Him."

Those words do not make sense if Jesus wills to reveal the Father to everyone. Clearly, the primary factor in whether or not a person knows God lies with Jesus' choice of that person, not with the person's choice of Jesus. To say anything different denies the plain statement of our Lord and exalts proud, fallen man. The Bible humbles the pride of man by showing that if God had not chosen to reveal Himself to you through His Word, you would be in complete spiritual darkness. You could not know Him at all!

The author of Hebrews directly says two more things about God's specific revelation in the Old Testament prophets, plus he implies a third fact. First, God spoke "in many portions." This refers to the 39 different books of the Old Testament: the law of Moses, the different prophets, and the writings, which included the poetic and historical books.

Second, God spoke "in many ways." Sometimes He revealed Himself through angels. He spoke to Moses through the burning bush, and later directly on the mountain. He revealed Himself to the Israelites through fire, thunder, earthquake, and clouds. He also revealed Himself through the miracles that He did through Moses. He spoke to Isaiah in the vision of His glory and to Ezekiel in the vision of the wheels and living creatures. He sometimes used dreams, object lessons, natural events, and other means. All of these things are recorded in His written Word for our instruction.

Third, it is implied here that God's revelation in the Old Testament was progressive. All of it was true, but it was incomplete, or else there would have been no need for His final and complete revelation in His Son. The Old Testament was like a developing mosaic, with each part adding more until the totality pointed clearly to Jesus Christ. The picture continued to grow more clear, but it was not complete until the New Testament revealed Jesus Christ to us. Thus to understand the Old Testament correctly, we must view it through the completed revelation of the New Testament. God spoke in the past through His written Word.

2. In the present, God has spoken supremely and finally in His Son.

As the divine voice from heaven boomed on the Mount of Transfiguration (Luke 9:35), "This is My Son, My Chosen One; listen to Him!" The Greek phrase, "in these last days," is found in the Septuagint, where it often refers to the day of Messiah. F. F. Bruce (p. 3) says,

> His word was not completely uttered until Christ came; but when Christ came, the word spoken in Him was indeed God's final word.... The story

of divine revelation is a story of progression up to Christ, but there is no progression beyond Him.

So in Christ there is both continuity and contrast. The continuity is that God spoke through the prophets and God spoke through Christ. But the contrast is, the prophets were many and fragmentary; Christ was one and complete. The prophets were all sinners; Jesus alone was perfectly holy. The prophets were preparatory; Jesus is the final fulfillment.

There is also a contrast of being. The prophets were mere men, but Jesus was God's Son. In the Greek, there is no word "His" and no definite article before "Son." The construction emphasizes the Son's essential nature (Morris, *ibid.*). Jesus is the Son of God in two aspects: eternally, He is the Son, one with the Father, the second person of the Trinity. Temporally, He is God's Son incarnate, born of the virgin Mary, taking on our human nature so that He could bear our sins (Luke 1:38). It is in this second aspect that He is referred to here. Jesus, who is eternal God in human flesh, supremely and finally reveals God to us.

A. W. Pink (*An Exposition of Hebrews* [electronic ed.] Ephesians Four Group: Escondido, CA, p. 27) explains the use of Son here this way:

> Were a friend to tell you that he had visited a certain church, and that the preacher "spoke in Latin," you would have no difficulty in understanding what he meant: "spoke *in* Latin" would intimate that that particular language marked his utterance. Such is the thought here. "In Son" has reference to that which **characterised** God's revelation. The thought of the contrast is that God, who of old had spoken **prophetwise**, now speaks **sonwise**.

Why did the author mention Jesus' Sonship without mentioning Him by name (he doesn't use Jesus' name until 2:9)? Perhaps these Jewish believers, under pressure, were tempted to deny the Trinity and go back to the strong Jewish unitarianism. He will go on immediately to show that the Son is the eternal Creator and that the Old Testament affirms Him to be God (1:2, 8). To go back to their old way of thinking would be to turn their backs on God's supreme, complete, and final revelation of Himself in His Son. To deny the Trinity is to deny the very being of God!

Conclusion

I conclude with three applications: *First, we should interpret the Bible Christologically.* That is to say, we must understand the Old Testament to be looking forward to fulfillment in Jesus Christ. The New Testament shows us how He is the complete and final revelation of God to us. Christ fulfills the Old Testament types. He is God's final and sufficient sacrifice for our sins. The Old Testament law is our tutor to bring us to Christ (Gal. 3:24). Many Old Testament prophecies point ahead to Him. All of this implies that if you do not read and study the Old Testament, you will miss much that God is saying to you (Rom. 15:4; 1 Cor. 10:1-11).

Second, we should not look for or expect any new revelation from God after the completion of the New Testament. Anyone who claims to have further revelation is a false prophet. This includes everyone from Mohammed and the Koran to Joseph Smith and the Book of Mormon to Mary Baker Eddy and her teachings. God has spoken definitively and finally in the Old and New Testaments which point to Jesus Christ, His Son.

Finally, if we are not using the Bible to come to know Jesus Christ in a deeper, more personal way, we are not using it correctly. That is not to say that we should not study theology, Bible history, prophecy, and many other biblically related subjects. But it is to say that our study of all these areas should lead us to know Christ better and to submit more completely to Him. As the title of a book by W. H. Griffith Thomas put it, *Christianity is Christ* [Moody Press]. After beginning by pointing out that no other world religion rests on the person of its founder, he states (p. 6), "Christianity is nothing less and can be nothing more than relationship to Christ."

And so the most crucial question in life for every person is the one Jesus asked the disciples (Matt. 16:15), "Who do you say that I am?" The Book of Hebrews will help us to grow in our understanding of that question as we consider Jesus (3:1). If you've never heard God speak, bow before Him and ask Him to reveal Himself to you through His Son, as revealed in His written Word.

Application Questions

1. Why is the correct identity of the person of Jesus Christ the most important question in life? How would you answer a critic who said that the gospels are fabrications about Jesus?

2. Why is philosophy useless when it comes to knowing God?

3. Does God give any extra-biblical revelation in our day? How can we evaluate such claims ("I have a word from God," etc.)?

4. What pressures tempt you to abandon Christ and go back to the world? How (practically) can knowing Him more fully strengthen us to stand firm in the face of trials?

Hebrews 1:2b-3, New American Standard Bible 1995

2 ... whom He appointed heir of all things, through whom also He made the world. 3 And He is the radiance of His glory and the exact representation of His nature, and upholds all things by the word of His power. When He had made purification of sins, He sat down at the right hand of the Majesty on high, ...

The Supremacy of the Son
Hebrews 1:2b-3

Have you ever visited the Canadian Rockies, near Banff and Lake Louise? If you have been there, you know that it has some of the most spectacular scenery in the world. Marla and I have visited there three times, and we've always been awestruck by the magnificent beauty of the glacier-capped mountains and turquoise lakes. Each evening that we camped at Lake Louise, we drove over to a viewpoint to watch the hour-long sunset that began around 9 p.m. It is difficult *not* to feel close to God in a place like that, as you drink in the handiwork of His creation!

If gazing on beautiful scenery causes us to rejoice in our glorious Creator, then gazing on the Lord Jesus Christ should cause us to worship even more so. Creation reveals God's "invisible attributes, His eternal power and divine nature" (Rom. 1:20). But God's Son is "the radiance of His glory and the exact representation of His nature" (Heb. 1:3).

My verbal description of the beauty of the Canadian Rockies is woefully inadequate. At least once in your life, I hope that you can go there and drink in what God has made, because you have to experience it personally to appreciate it. Likewise, my feeble attempts in this chapter to describe the glory of the Lord Jesus Christ are going to be deficient. I hope that you will not only carefully read what I say, but also that you will take the time personally to visit these verses over and over again, asking God to reveal more of the beauty of His Son to your soul!

In the last chapter I said that the most crucial question for every person to answer is Jesus' question to the disciples, "Who do you say that I am?" *Everything* hangs on the correct answer to that question! If you are mistaken about Jesus' identity, you will not bow before Him as Lord and Savior, and you will spend eternity in hell. That is why the cults, such as the Mormons and Jehovah's Witnesses, are so destructive. They mislead and deceive people about the person of Jesus Christ.

If you answer that question correctly, you will recognize that Jesus is King of kings and Lord of lords, the only One who can save you from your sins. You will fall down before Him in adoration and praise. You will yield yourself totally

The Supremacy of the Son

to Him in love and live to glorify Him. You will spend eternity with Him, singing with all of the angels and saints (Rev. 5:12), "Worthy is the Lamb that was slain...." As Jesus told Peter after he answered that question, the correct answer cannot come from any human source. The Father in heaven must reveal it to you (Matt. 16:17). So pause right now and ask God to reveal the supremacy of His Son to your soul.

Our text continues the opening sentence of Hebrews. The author is showing that Jesus Christ is God's supreme and final revelation to us. All the Old Testament prophets pointed ahead to Christ. The New Testament reveals that God's eternal purpose is to sum up all things in Christ (see Eph. 1:10-12).

Now the author unfolds seven brief, but profoundly packed phrases that reveal the supremacy of God's Son. Together they reveal the threefold office of Christ as God's *Prophet*, revealing His final word; God's *Priest*, who made purification for our sins; and God's *King*, who is enthroned at the right hand of the Majesty on high. The arrangement of these seven statements may be chiastic, with the first and last statements speaking of the Son in His incarnation and the clauses in between speaking of the Son in His eternal existence (Philip Edgcumbe Hughes, *A Commentary on the Epistle to the Hebrews* [Eerdmans], p. 49).

Although there is some deep theology here about the relationship between the Father and the Son, I was a bit surprised to find John Calvin emphasize that the point of the author is not theological, but practical (*Calvin's Commentaries* [Baker reprint], on Hebrews 1:3, pp. 35-36): "His purpose was really to build up our faith, so that we may learn that God is made known to us in no other way than in Christ: for as to the essence of God, so immense is the brightness that it dazzles our eyes, except it shines on us in Christ." The practical import of our text is:

Since God's Son is supreme over all, we must bow before Him as the Sovereign Lord.

Let's consider the seven phrases that reveal His supremacy:

1. Jesus is supreme as the heir of all things.

As the Son, Jesus is also the heir. The early church fathers and the medieval writers associated this statement with Psalm 2:8, where the Father says to the Son, "Ask of Me, and I will surely give the nations as Your inheritance, and the very ends of the earth as Your possession" (P. Hughes, p. 39). Thus it speaks of Christ in His role as Redeemer and as Lord over the nations in His kingdom. Leon Morris (*The Expositor's Bible Commentary*, ed. by Frank Gaebelein [Zondervan], 12:13) says that *heir of all things* "is a title of dignity and shows that Christ has the supreme place in all the mighty universe. His exaltation to the highest place in heaven after his work on earth was done did not mark some new dignity but his reentry into his right place (cf. Phil. 2:6-11)."

Calvin (p. 34) says that the word heir is ascribed to Christ in His humanity "for this purpose, that he might restore to us what we had lost in Adam." Calvin applies this truth by saying (p. 33), "It hence follows that we must be very miserable and destitute of all good things except he supplies us with his treasures." As Paul proclaims, if we are in Christ as His children, we are heirs with Him (Rom. 8:15-18; Gal. 4:4-7). All that is His is ours! We will someday share His glory throughout eternity!

But you only share in Christ's inheritance if you are in Him through faith. If you have not applied the purification of sins that He obtained to your sinful heart by faith, then you are not His child and you do not share in His inheritance. Make sure that your trust is in Him alone!

But many of His children are only vaguely aware of their inheritance. Thus, we should pray for one another and for ourselves (Eph. 1:18), that "the Father of glory may give to [us] a spirit of wisdom and of revelation in the knowledge of Him," that the eyes of our hearts would be enlightened, "so that [we] will know what is the hope of His calling, what are the riches of the glory of His inheritance in the saints."

2. Jesus is supreme as the creator of all things.

"Through whom also He made the world." *World* is literally *ages* in the Greek text. Here it refers to "the whole created universe of space and time" (F. F. Bruce, *Commentary on the Epistle to the Hebrews* [Eerdmans], p. 4). It means that Jesus is Lord over time and all that has been created in time, because He created it. As John 1:3 asserts, "All things came into being through Him, and apart from Him nothing came into being that has come into being." Or, as Paul puts it (Rom. 11:36), "For from Him and through Him and to Him are all things. To Him be the glory forever. Amen."

These affirmations show that Jesus Christ is eternal God, one with the Father before time began. Athanasius, who contended against the Arian heresy (whose modern counterpart is the Jehovah's Witnesses), said that when the sacred writers affirmed that Jesus created the world, "they proclaim the eternal and everlasting being of the Son and thereby designate him as God" (in P. Hughes, p. 40). The Jehovah's Witnesses latch onto Colossians 1:15, where Paul refers to Jesus as God's "firstborn." They say that the term means that Jesus was created, not eternal. But they fail to notice that verse 16 explains ("For") the term in verse 15: "For by Him all things were created, both in the heavens and on earth, visible and invisible, whether thrones or dominions or rulers or authorities—all things have been created through Him and for Him." "Firstborn" is not a chronological term, but has to do with the legal rights of authority and inheritance. The fact that the Father created all things through Jesus shows that Jesus is Almighty God!

Think of the intricacies of the atom, or the mysteries of human and animal DNA, which modern science only barely understands. It all reflects amazing design, and that design is often interdependent, so that you can't have only part of it. The parts depend on the design of other parts that work in harmony. Or, consider the immensity of the universe. Our galaxy is just an average-sized galaxy that takes 100,000 light years to cross (600 trillion miles). Modern telescopes can see about 100,000 million galaxies, with each galaxy containing 100,000 million stars. The average distance between these galaxies is three million light years. Some estimate that the most distant galaxy is about eight billion light years away! (These figures are in R. Kent Hughes, *Hebrews: An Anchor for the Soul* [Crossway Books], 1:27, citing Stephen Hawking, *A Brief History of Time* [Bantam], pp. 37-39.) Jesus spoke all of this into existence out of nothing (Heb. 11:3; Gen. 1:1)!

3. Jesus is supreme as the radiance of the Father's glory.

The early church fathers often used this verse to refute the heretics, especially the Arians. Theodoret says that the Arians rejected Hebrews from the canon because of this text (P. Hughes, p. 41). This statement and the next, that Jesus is "the exact representation of His nature," reflect both the oneness of the Son with the Father and yet His distinctness from the Father. Thus the two phrases fit together and balance each other (P. Hughes, *ibid.*).

The ascription of Jesus as "the radiance of His glory" pictures the rays of the sun displaying its brilliance. Jesus, of course, reflects the Father's glory, but also possesses an inherent glory of His own, as seen on the Mount of Transfiguration and by John in Revelation 1. Athanasius asks, "Who does not see that the brightness cannot be separated from the light, but that it is by nature proper to it and co-existent with it, and is not produced after it?" Ambrose explains, "Where there is light there is radiance, and where there is radiance there is also light; and thus we cannot have a light without radiance nor radiance without light, because both the light is in the radiance and the radiance in the light" (both citations in P. Hughes, p. 42).

In other words, "the Son is co-eternal with the Father, just as brightness is coeval with the sun.... The Son exists essentially in the Father and the Father in the Son" (Herveus, in P. Hughes, p. 43). The reason it is important to affirm this, as Athanasius saw, is "that a false doctrine of the person of Christ must inevitably result in a false doctrine of the work of Christ and consequently undermine the whole system of the gospel" (P. Hughes, *ibid.*).

4. Jesus is supreme as the exact representation of the Father's nature.

The Greek word translated *exact representation* refers to the engraved character or impression made by a die or a seal as, for example, on a coin. The word translated *nature* "denotes the very essence of God. The principal idea intended is that of exact correspondence. This correspondence involves not only an identity of the essence of the Son with that of the Father, but more particularly a true and trustworthy revelation or representation of the Father by the Son" (P. Hughes, *ibid.*). As Jesus told Philip (John 14:9), "He who has seen Me has seen the Father." To know God, we must know Him as He is revealed to us by the Son (Luke 10:22).

While these terms express some deep theology concerning the nature of the Trinity, and thus were rightly used by the church fathers to defend the faith against destructive heresies, we should not forget Calvin's point, that these terms teach that we can only know God through Christ. We never could have understood the God "who dwells in unapproachable light, whom no man has seen or can see" (1 Tim. 6:16), unless Jesus had come to earth as a man to reveal Him.

The story is told of a devout Hindu man who was confronted with the claims of Christ. But he could not grasp the concept that God had taken on human flesh in the person of Jesus. This Hindu regarded all of life, including insects, as sacred. One day as he walked in a field wrestling with the concept of God becoming man, he came upon an anthill with thousands of ants. This anthill was in the path of a farmer plowing the field.

Gripped with a concern that you or I would feel for hundreds of people trapped in a burning building, he wanted to warn them of their impending destruction. But, how? He could shout to them, but they would not hear. He could write in the sand, but they would not understand. How could he communicate with them? Then it dawned on him: if he only could become an ant, he could warn them before it was too late. Now he understood the Christian message, that God became a man in Jesus to communicate to us His message of salvation (*Teacher's Manual for the Ten Basic Steps Toward Christian Maturity* [Campus Crusade for Christ], pp. 18-19).

Thus we've seen that Jesus is supreme as the *heir* of all things; as the *creator* of all things; as the *radiance* of the Father's glory; and, as the *exact representation* of His nature. Next,

5. Jesus is supreme as the sustainer of all things by the word of His power.

This phrase refers to Christ's "carrying forward and onward of all things to the predestined consummation which is also implicit in their beginning" (P. Hughes, p. 45). It refers to His sustaining providence and governance of all things (*ibid.*). "It does not simply mean 'sustain,' but has the sense of active, purposeful control…" (Wayne Grudem, *Systematic Theology* [Zondervan], p. 316). The use of the present participle in our text indicates that Jesus is *continually* upholding all things in the universe by His word of power (*ibid.*). If He ceased from doing this, the universe would disintegrate! Paul states the same truth when he says, "in Him all things hold together" (Col. 1:17).

This refutes the idea of Deism, that God created all things, but then bowed out and let everything run on its own. Scripture shows that there is not a single atom in the universe that acts apart from God's providential governance. Every raindrop, snowflake, gust of wind, and lightning bolt obey God's command (Ps. 148:8). He directs everything from the roll of the dice (Prov. 16:33) to the rise and fall of nations (Job 12:23). He determines in advance the number of days that each of us will live (Ps. 139:16). Our text says that Jesus exercises this immense power simply by speaking, or as Calvin says (p. 38), "with a nod." This means that there is no such thing as random chance or luck. We are totally dependent on God, and we must receive all things as coming from Him according to His purpose for our good (Gen. 50:20; Job 2:10; Rom. 8:28).

6. Jesus is supreme as the One who made purification for our sins.

The juxtaposition of Christ's upholding all things by the word of His power and the next phrase, "when He had made purification of sins," is stunning! The almighty Lord who could simply "let go" and sinners would disintegrate, instead left the glory of heaven, took on the form of a servant, and became obedient to death, even death on a cross, to purify us from our sins (Phil. 2:5-11)! "Amazing love, how can it be, that Thou my God shouldst die for me" (Charles Wesley)!

The Greek aorist tense indicates that Jesus accomplished purification for sins once and for all. The author will expound on this further in chapter 10. Jesus did not just make purification of sins *possible*, but *effectual* through His death on the cross (see 10:10, 12, 14, 18). What I am about to say here is controversial, but I ask you to consider it and ask God for understanding. I believe that on the cross, Jesus did not actually make purification of sins for all people. If He did, all would be purified, and everyone would go to heaven. Rather, He actually secured purification of sins for all that the Father had given to Him (John 6:38-39).

C. H. Spurgeon put it this way when he preached on this text (*Metropolitan Tabernacle Pulpit* [Pilgrim Publications], 45:393):

> I tremble when I hear some people talk about the disappointed Christ,— or about his having died at a peradventure, to accomplish he knew not what,— dying for something which the will of man might give him if it would, but it might possibly be denied him. I buy nothing on such terms

as that, I expect to have what I purchase; and Christ will have what he bought with his own blood; especially as he lives again to claim his purchase.

It is of great comfort to know that our purification is secure because Christ paid for us, and He will get what He paid for!

7. Jesus is supreme as the One who sat down at the right hand of the Majesty on high.

Christ's sitting signifies the *completion of the work of redemption*. In the Old Testament, the priests always stood in the Holy of Holies when making atonement. But Jesus offered Himself for our sins once for all and took His seat on high. His sitting at the right hand of the Majesty on high (a reverent term for God) also signifies His being in *the place of highest honor*. This is not a literal place, in that God, who is Spirit, does not have a right hand or left. But it uses human language to convey that there is no higher designation possible! Sitting at the right hand of God also pictures Jesus as the *Sovereign Ruler* of the universe (1:8, 13).

While this phrase affirms Jesus' deity (how could any created being sit at the right hand of the Majesty on high without being consumed?), it also indicates a degree of subordination of the Son to the Father (P. Hughes, p. 48). Though equal with God in His essential being, the Son voluntarily submits to the Father to carry out the divine purpose (1 Cor. 15:24-28). Paul uses this order in the Godhead to argue for the leadership of men over women in the local church (1 Cor. 11:3-16). Men and women are equal in their being and as heirs with Christ, but there is to be an order of headship and submission to reflect the image of God.

Conclusion

When I went to Coast Guard Boot Camp, we were pretty much on our own for the first weekend, which was a holiday. But in our barracks was the office of the most ill-named man I have ever met, Mr. Angel. This man's reputation went before him and grew bigger up to the first moment that he strode into the barracks and sent terror into every heart. We had heard that he was meanness personified. For recreation, he liked to go into bars and pick fights. A sign on his door said that before he was through with you, you would know his shoe size from intimate contact with your behind. He reputedly marched one company off the end of a pier into the water to see if they would obey his commands.

So when Mr. Angel stomped into our barracks and barked, "On your feet, squirrels!" (plus a few unrepeatable expletives), there was not a single man who stayed on his bunk and said, "I don't feel like getting on my feet just now!" The point is, because Mr. Angel had authority to do you great bodily harm, you obeyed his every command! Whatever Mr. Angel commanded, we did with great haste!

I hope that you see that this glorious description of our Lord Jesus Christ is not just interesting theology, but that it applies practically to every one of us. If Jesus Christ is who the writer here proclaims Him to be, then we all must bow before Him in worship and obey His every claim on our lives. To brazenly disobey the Sovereign, Almighty Creator and Lord of the universe would be utterly arrogant and stupid! God's Son is supreme over all. We must live to obey Him completely!

Application Questions

1. Why is our understanding of who Jesus is so vitally important?
2. The Jehovah's Witnesses say that Jesus is the highest created being. Can a person believe this and be saved? Why not?
3. How can we know that the claims of Christ are genuine and not made up later by His followers?
4. Can any for whom Jesus made purification of sins reject Him and be lost? Defend biblically.

Hebrews 1:4-14, New American Standard Bible 1995

4 ... having become as much better than the angels, as He has inherited a more excellent name than they.

5 For to which of the angels did He ever say,

"You are My Son,

Today I have begotten You"?

And again,

"I will be a Father to Him

And He shall be a Son to Me"?

6 And when He again brings the firstborn into the world, He says,

"And let all the angels of God worship Him."

7 And of the angels He says,

"Who makes His angels winds,

And His ministers a flame of fire."

8 But of the Son He says,

"Your throne, O God, is forever and ever,

And the righteous scepter is the scepter of His kingdom.

9 "You have loved righteousness and hated lawlessness;

Therefore God, Your God, has anointed You

With the oil of gladness above Your companions."

10 And,

"You, Lord, in the beginning laid the foundation of the earth,

And the heavens are the works of Your hands;

11 They will perish, but You remain;

And they all will become old like a garment,

12 And like a mantle You will roll them up;

Like a garment they will also be changed.

But You are the same,

And Your years will not come to an end."

13 But to which of the angels has He ever said,

"Sit at My right hand,

Until I make Your enemies

A footstool for Your feet"?

14 Are they not all ministering spirits, sent out to render service for the sake of those who will inherit salvation?

The Son's Supremacy Over Angels
Hebrews 1:4-14

A few years ago, the *Chicago Tribune* reported the story of a woman in New Mexico who was frying tortillas when she noticed that the skillet burns on one of her tortillas resembled the face of Jesus. She excitedly showed it to her husband and neighbors, who all agreed that the face etched on the tortilla truly bore a resemblance to Jesus.

The woman went to her priest to have the tortilla blessed. She testified that the tortilla had changed her life, and her husband agreed that she had become more peaceful, happy, and submissive since the tortilla had arrived. The priest was a bit reluctant, not being accustomed to blessing tortillas. But he agreed to do it.

The woman took the tortilla home, put it in a glass case with piles of cotton to make it look like it was floating on clouds, built a special altar for it, and opened the little shrine to visitors. Within a few months, more than 8,000 people came to the "Shrine of Jesus the Tortilla." All of them agreed that the face in the burn marks on the tortilla was the face of Jesus, except for one reporter, who said he thought it looked like former heavyweight boxing champion, Leon Spinks.

We may laugh at that story, but to be mistaken about the person of Jesus Christ is no laughing matter. As we've seen in the past two studies, the most crucial question for each person to answer correctly is Jesus' question to His disciples, "Who do you say that I am?" (Matt. 16:15). If we have an inadequate or incorrect view of who Jesus is, we will not bow before Him and trust in Him as Savior and Lord. Thus our eternal destiny rides on correctly understanding the person and work of Jesus Christ.

Since this is such a crucial matter, it is not surprising that Satan has launched repeated attacks against the person of Christ. Sometimes the attacks have denied Jesus' true humanity. At other times (far more frequently in our skeptical day), he undermines the true deity of Jesus. One of his most dangerous tricks is to lower Jesus just "slightly" below the status of God. Thus the Jehovah's Witnesses teach that Jesus is "a god," and even "a mighty god," but not God Almighty. They teach that Jesus was created

The Son's Supremacy Over Angels

as the archangel Michael and that through him, all other things in the universe were created. Thus they hold to a relatively high view of Jesus, but they deny His full deity. But as Bishop Moule once said, "A Savior not quite God is a bridge broken at the farther end."

Satan has used the same tricks to deceive people for centuries. After one trick gets old, he puts it back into his bag and saves it to bring it out later when everyone has forgotten it. Holding to wrong views of angels in relation to Jesus Christ is such a trick. The Jewish Christians to whom our author was writing were tempted by teaching that elevated angels to a position that rivaled or even surpassed that of Jesus Christ Himself.

We know that Paul warned the Colossian church about the early Gnostic heresy that included angel worship (Col. 2:18). It is debatable whether these views were in our author's mind when he wrote this section (Philip E. Hughes, *A Commentary on the Epistle to the Hebrews* [Eerdmans], p. 52). There was also a Jewish Dead Sea Sect, which believed in a dual messiah, both of whom would be subject to the archangel Michael (P. Hughes, pp. 14, 53). These views may have infiltrated this Jewish church.

Also, the Jews at this time had begun to embellish the Old Testament teaching on angels (John MacArthur, *The MacArthur New Testament Commentary, Hebrews* [Moody Press], pp. 24-25). The Bible says that the Old Testament Law was ordained through angels (Acts 7:53; Gal. 3:19), and it shows that they are impressive and important beings. So if our author was going to convince his readers that Jesus is supreme over Judaism, he had to show how He was not only supreme over Moses, but also over the angels. He had to show them that Jesus' becoming a man did not place Him beneath the angels in terms of His essential nature as eternal God. In our text he shows (as other Scriptures teach, cf. Col. 1:16) that Jesus created the angels. His overall point here is that...

Jesus' superiority to the angels rests on the fact that He is God.

The author uses the Old Testament to prove his point, since his readers accepted its authority. He uses seven passages, all taken from the Septuagint (LXX = the Greek translation of the Hebrew Old Testament). We may group his arguments under five headings:

1. Jesus is superior to the angels because He is uniquely the Son of God (1:4-5).

The author says that Jesus has "become as much better than the angels, as He has inherited a more excellent name than they" (1:4). For the Hebrews, the name signified "the essential character of a person in himself and in his work" (P. Hughes, p. 50). In the sense of His eternal existence and His essential nature, Jesus *always* had a more excellent name than the angels.

But the statement here about His *having become* as much better than the angels refers to what Jesus accomplished through His incarnation, death on the cross for our sins, resurrection, and ascension into glory again. The name that is especially in view here is, "Son of God." While the angels were sometimes referred to in the plural as "sons of God" (Job 1:6), and while believers are called "sons of God" (John 1:12), no single angel or believer was ever referred to as "*the* Son of God." That title uniquely belongs to Jesus and signifies His deity, as the Jews themselves knew (John 5:18).

The author backs up the claim to Jesus' more excellent name by quoting the well known messianic Psalm 2:7, "You are My Son, today I have begotten You." In that psalm, the verse quoted here is preceded by the statement, "I will surely tell of the decree of the Lord." Because that decree took place in eternity, before creation, the church has affirmed the eternal Sonship of Jesus Christ and has said that He is "eternally begotten" by the Father, not made ("The Nicene Creed"). In other words, since God exists in eternity, begetting is not an event that took place in time. Rather, it describes an eternal relationship between the first and second members of the Godhead. They always have and always will relate to one another as Father and Son. Like a human father and son, God the Father and Jesus the Son share the same essential nature, which is the main point. Unlike a human father and son, God the Father did not pre-date the existence of God the Son, because Jesus shares His nature as eternal God (John 1:1-3).

But, in our text, the author omits the statement about the decree because, in conjunction with verse 4, his focus is more on the incarnational aspects of Jesus as the Son of God, than on the eternal aspects of that truth. Some relate "today" to Jesus' baptism, when the Father declared, "This is My beloved Son." Others relate it to Jesus' resurrection, which declared Him to be the Son of God with power (Rom. 1:4). Paul preached that Jesus' resurrection fulfilled Psalm 2:7, proving Him to be God's Son (Acts 13:33).

F. F. Bruce (*Commentary on the Epistle to the Hebrews* [Eerdmans], p. 13) relates "today" to the exaltation and enthronement of Christ, which is an emphasis throughout Hebrews. He explains that this does not in any way question the eternal Sonship of Christ. Rather, he says, "He who was the Son of God from everlasting entered into the full exercise of all the prerogatives implied by His Sonship when, after His suffering had proved the completeness of His obedience, He was raised to the Father's right hand" (*ibid.*).

The second quotation to back up Jesus as God's unique Son comes from 2 Samuel 7:14, where God promised David that He will be a Father to David's son, and "He shall be a Son to Me." That promise had an initial fulfillment in Solomon, who built the Temple, but its final fulfillment was in David's greater Son, the Lord Jesus Christ. As the angel told Mary (Luke 1:32, 33), "He will be great and will be called the Son of the Most High; and the Lord God will give Him the throne of His father David, and He will reign over the house of Jacob forever, and His kingdom will have no end."

Thus the author's first point is that Jesus is greater than the angels because of His unique position as the Son of God, as seen in two Old Testament prophecies. To demote Him to the level of the angels, who are mere messengers (1:14), would be blasphemy!

2. Jesus is superior to the angels because they worship and serve Him (1:6-7).

Hebrews 1:6-7:

> "And when He again brings the firstborn into the world, He says,
>   'And let all the angels of God worship Him.'
> And of the angels He says,
>   'Who makes His angels winds,
>   And His ministers a flame of fire.'

The overall point of these verses is clear, that the angels worship and serve Jesus, not vice versa. But there are several details that require explanation.

First, the author refers to Jesus as God's *firstborn*. To our minds, firstborn sounds like a chronological concept, that someone was born first in time in a family. But for the Hebrews, firstborn signified position, not time. The oldest son was *usually*, but not always, the heir to the father's estate. As such, he was in a position of privilege and preeminence over his brothers. The title is used in Psalm 89:27, where God says of David, "I shall also make him My firstborn, the highest of the kings of the earth." David was not the firstborn son of Jesse. In fact, he was the youngest son. But he was the most prestigious and preeminent son, because God had chosen him above his brothers.

If "firstborn" meant what the Jehovah's Witnesses say it means, that Jesus was the first one created, then why would God command the angels to worship Jesus? To worship anyone less than God Himself would be blasphemy. Surely God would not command such a thing!

There are two other interpretive issues in verse 6. The first has to do with the adverb "again." Should it go at the front of the sentence, and thus mark the following quotation as yet another Scripture that sets forth the exalted position of Christ? Or, should it be connected with the verb "brings" (as in the NASB), thus pointing not to the first coming of Christ, but to His second coming? While some reputable scholars argue for the second view, the majority favor the first view (P. Hughes, p. 58). It is not a major issue, in that all who believe in Jesus would agree that the angels worshiped Him when He came to earth the first time (Luke 2:13-14) and that they will worship Him when He comes again (Rev. 5:11-12).

The other issue in verse 6 is the source of the quote. It is similar, but not exact, to Psalm 97:7 [96:7] in the LXX. But it is verbatim from the LXX of Deuteronomy 32:43. The problem is, this line in the LXX is not in the Hebrew Bible. But it has been found in one of the Dead Sea Scrolls, and so perhaps was original.

The main point of verse 7 is that the angels belong to Jesus ("His angels") and that they obey His commands. Thus they are His servants, and not vice versa. Also, the terms "winds" and "fire" point to the transitory, changing nature of their service, as contrasted with the eternal sovereignty and glory of Christ, as portrayed in verse 8. The point is that Jesus is superior to the angels because they worship and serve Him.

The Son's Supremacy Over Angels

3. Jesus is superior to the angels because He is the God who reigns eternally (1:8-9).

Hebrews 1:8-9:

"But of the Son He says,
 'Your throne, O God, is forever and ever,
 And the righteous scepter is the scepter of His kingdom.
 'You have loved righteousness and hated lawlessness;
 Therefore God, Your God, has anointed You
 With the oil of gladness above Your companions.'"

Note the contrast between the angels (1:6-7) and the Son (1:8). Here the author quotes Psalm 45:6-7. This psalm celebrated a royal wedding, perhaps of King Solomon or one of David's other descendants (Bruce, p. 19), addressing the king as God. F. F. Bruce (*ibid.*) explains that this is not the only place in the Old Testament to use such hyperbolic language (see Isa. 9:6; Jer. 23:5-6). Some would translate it as, "God is your throne," but other than theological bias, there is no reason to do so. If someone objects to the Son being addressed as God in verse 8, they still have to contend with verse 10, where He is addressed as the Lord and Creator.

The author's clear point is that, as God, Jesus reigns forever and ever. His rule is marked by the love of righteousness and the hatred of lawlessness. These qualities marked Jesus' earthly life and ministry, and they will supremely mark His coming kingdom, when He rules the nations with a rod of iron (Rev. 19:15). The oil of gladness refers to His triumph over sin and death and His return to His rightful glory. The "companions" may refer to angels, but more likely refers to the "many sons" that He brings to glory through His suffering and resurrection (2:10, 11). Note also that righteousness and joy always go together. It is Satan's lie that righteousness is boring! In God's holy presence are fullness of joy and pleasures forever (Ps. 16:11).

Thus Jesus is superior to the angels because He is uniquely the Son of God; because they worship and serve Him; and, because He is the God who reigns eternally.

4. Jesus is superior to the angels because He is the eternal Creator of heaven and earth (1:10-12).

Hebrews 1:10-12:

"And,

> 'You, Lord, in the beginning laid the foundation of the earth,
> And the heavens are the works of Your hands;
> They will perish, but You remain;
> And they all will become old like a garment,
> And like a mantle You will roll them up;
> Like a garment they will also be changed.
> But You are the same,
> And Your years will not come to an end.'"

This sixth quotation is taken from Psalm 102:25-27, which begins, "A prayer of the afflicted when he is faint and pours out his complaint before the Lord." The psalmist has gone through some difficult trials, which he describes in strong poetic language in the first part of the psalm. He feels as if he is about to be taken away in the midst of his days. But in his weakness and desperation, he considers the eternality, power, and unchangeableness of the Lord as Creator. He says that even though heaven and earth will perish, God remains. Like a man throws away old clothes, God will throw away the universe, but He remains the same, and His years will never come to an end.

The remarkable thing about the quote is that in the psalm, these verses clearly describe Almighty God, and yet the author of Hebrews applies them directly to Jesus. Oscar Cullman observed (in P. Hughes, p. 68), "We should generally give much more consideration to the by no means self-evident fact that after the death of Jesus the first Christians without hesitation transferred to him what the Old Testament says about God."

To this Jewish church, these words were not just a theological statement about Jesus' superiority to the angels. They were also meant to be a source of great comfort in the midst of trials. The same eternal Creator who sustained the psalmist in the midst of his calamity would sustain them in the midst of their troubles. And that eternal Creator is none other than their Lord and Savior, Jesus Christ! He is the same yesterday, today, and forever (Heb. 13:8). Even if you are taken away in the midst of your days, you have a lasting refuge in the eternal, unchanging Lord Jesus Christ!

The Son's Supremacy Over Angels

5. Jesus is superior to the angels because He sits at God's right hand, whereas they are sent out to serve the saints (1:13-14).

Hebrews 1:13-14:

"But to which of the angels has He ever said,

'Sit at My right hand,

Until I make Your enemies

A footstool for Your feet'?

Are they not all ministering spirits, sent out to render service for the sake of those who will inherit salvation?"

Verse 13 introduces the seventh quote with a rhetorical question: "But to which of the angels has He ever said, 'Sit at My right hand until I make Your enemies a footstool for Your feet'?" The implied answer is, None! The quote comes from Psalm 110:1, which is cited in the New Testament more often than any other Old Testament verse (14 times). Jesus used these verses to stump the Pharisees. He asked them, "Whose son is the Messiah?" They correctly answered, "The son of David." Then Jesus asked, "Then how does David in the Spirit call Him 'Lord,'" and quoted this verse. His clinching question was, "If David then calls Him 'Lord,' how is He his son?" (Matt. 22:42-45).

As we saw in verse 3, Jesus' exaltation to the right hand of the Majesty on high affirms His supreme authority and lordship. No created being could occupy that place. In the Bible, when men encountered angels, they often fell before them in fear and obeisance, but invariably the angel did not accept such worship, claiming, "I am a fellow servant... worship God" (Rev. 19:10). But even when He was on this earth with His glory veiled, Jesus accepted and encouraged those who fell before Him in worship (Luke 5:8-10; John 9:35-39; 20:26-29). How much more should we worship Him who now sits on the throne of God! How blasphemous it is of the Jehovah's Witnesses to say that Jesus is a created being, an angel! As verse 14 states, the angels are "ministering spirits, sent out to render service for the sake of those who will inherit salvation." To mistake Jesus for an angel is to mix up the Lord with His servants!

The descriptions of angels in the Bible show that they are impressive beings. In Genesis, two angels rescued Lot and his family from Sodom and then called down fire and brimstone from heaven on the wicked cities. On another occasion, an angel struck down 70,000 in Israel on account of David's sin (2 Sam. 24:15-17). One angel went out into the camp of Sennacherib's army and struck down 185,000 soldiers in a night (Isa. 37:36). An angel shut the lions' mouths so that Daniel was kept safe, and an angel revealed to Daniel the amazing prophecies of things to come. When Daniel saw the angel, it wiped out his strength and took his breath away (Dan. 6:22; 9:20-27; 10:17). An angel delivered Peter from prison and then struck the proud Herod Agrippa, so that he was eaten by worms and died (Acts 12:3-23).

The Bible teaches that angels guard believers (2 Kings 6:15-18; Ps. 91:11-12; Matt. 18:10) and look in on our church services (1 Cor. 11:10), although we are not able to see them. And yet, as great and powerful as angels are, they are just servants who stand before Him who sits at the right hand of the Majesty on high! Worship Him alone, because He is Almighty God!

Conclusion

I want to encourage you to apply this message in two ways. First, *if anyone tries to persuade you that Jesus is not fully God, recognize it as a temptation that comes straight from Satan!* He is currently deceiving a billion people worldwide with the lie that Jesus was a great prophet, but that He is not God (Islam). Even in our country, millions think that Jesus was a good man and a great moral teacher, but they do not bow before Him as Savior and Lord. All of these lies lead people into hell. If He was not God in human flesh, His sacrifice could not atone for our sins. He is the only way for us to know God and have our sins forgiven. Hold firmly to His absolute deity!

Second, I want to challenge all of you to do something that may be outside your comfort zone: *Buy and read a good systematic theology to ground yourself in the doctrines of our faith.* It is to our shame that most Jehovah's Witnesses can run circles around evangelical Christians when it comes to knowing their Bibles. Granted, they do not know their Bibles correctly (and they use a faulty translation), and they pervert the truth. But could you refute them from your Bible?

We live in a day that despises doctrine and opts for experiences and feelings. But if our experiences are not resting on solid truth, they are planted in air! Our lives must be founded on the truths of God's Word. The practical

The Son's Supremacy Over Angels

sections of Romans, Ephesians, Colossians, and Hebrews all follow chapters establishing solid doctrine.

I recommend Wayne Grudem's *Systematic Theology* [Zondervan] or the abridged edition, *Bible Doctrine*. There is a good one-volume abridged version of Charles Hodge's *Systematic Theology* [Baker]. Or, although it is not a systematic theology, read Calvin's *Institutes of the Christian Religion* [Westminster] (get the version edited by John McNeill and translated by Ford Lewis Battles). As Calvin himself believed, the aim of theology is not head knowledge, but godliness that stems from knowing God (see McNeill's introduction, pp. li, lii). Just five pages a day will get you through the whole thing in less than a year. Ask God to deepen your knowledge of Him and our exalted, divine Savior, the Lord Jesus Christ!

Application Questions

1. Why is it absolutely essential to the Christian faith to affirm the full deity of Jesus Christ?

2. A Jehovah's Witness tells you that "firstborn" means that Jesus is not eternal, but created. What Scriptures would you use to refute him?

3. Does God still use angels to minister to His saints? Are most "angel encounters" today genuine or counterfeit? How can we evaluate such encounters?

4. Why must sound doctrine be the basis of our Christian experience? How can we counter the anti-doctrinal bias of our day?

Hebrews 2:1-4, New American Standard Bible 1995

2 For this reason we must pay much closer attention to what we have heard, so that we do not drift away from it. 2 For if the word spoken through angels proved unalterable, and every transgression and disobedience received a just penalty, 3 how will we escape if we neglect so great a salvation? After it was at the first spoken through the Lord, it was confirmed to us by those who heard, 4 God also testifying with them, both by signs and wonders and by various miracles and by gifts of the Holy Spirit according to His own will.

The Danger of Drifting Spiritually
Hebrews 2:1-4

In 2003, I read that the Tour de France bicycle champion, Lance Armstrong, and his wife were divorcing. The article stated that at that point, he did not have another woman in his life. Rather, his many hours spent pursuing his bicycle career had left no time for his marriage.

Maybe I'm wrong, but I hope that in hindsight, Armstrong might say, "I was a fool to sacrifice my family for my sport!" But at the time, the fame and fortune blinded him to the more satisfying value of a lasting, loving marriage.

It's easy in life to get caught up in matters that seem very important at the time, but in the light of eternity will shrink into oblivion. Because we all have only so many hours in our day, our focus on these seemingly important matters also means that we neglect matters that are huge in light of eternity. When these things nag at our consciences, as invariably they do, we justify our current priorities by saying, "Someday I will attend to these eternally important matters, but right now, I'm too busy." But such procrastination can be eternally fatal!

The one sure fact of human existence is death. As George Bernard Shaw observed, "The statistics on death are quite impressive: one out of one people die!" Since we all have to face death, you would think that we all would live in view of eternity, but we don't. Other pressing matters come up to divert our attention: "I've got to get through school." "I've got to get established in my career." "I've got to get the kids raised, and then I'll have some time." Many of these pressing matters are good and important, but they easily can crowd out the most important thing. As a result, even we who know the truth of the gospel are always in danger of drifting spiritually.

The author of Hebrews has spent the first chapter extolling the supremacy of the Son of God, the Lord Jesus Christ. He has not mentioned a word of application or exhortation to this point. But now, as a concerned pastor, he pauses in his argument to apply what he has written. Our text is the first of five warning sections in this letter. These warnings are addressed to professing Christians who were in the church. By using the first-person plural pronoun, "we," the author identifies himself with his readers. He faced the same temptations that they faced. He was not in an ivory tower, exempt from these pitfalls.

Like every faithful pastor, he was exhorting himself first, even as he exhorted his congregation.

The danger that he was confronting was this: *You are either drifting with regard to your salvation because of neglect, or you are growing because of deliberate effort and attention.* But *nobody* grows by accident.

Since we have encountered such a great salvation, we must be careful not to drift away from it.

There are three main points:

1. The salvation Christ offers is indescribably great.

He calls it "so great a salvation" (2:3). He gives us four reasons that this salvation is indescribably great.

    A. Salvation is great because it is the one thing that every person needs more than anything else.

In church circles we toss around the word "salvation" so often that it loses its true meaning. But verse 3 contains another word to alert us to the significance of the concept: "escape." "How shall we escape…?" An escape points to a situation of great peril. You don't need to be saved unless you are in grave danger of perishing. If our soldiers rescue a prisoner of war from hostile enemies, they *save* him so that he *escapes* further torture and perhaps death.

Outside of Jesus Christ, every sinner (that is, every person, since all have sinned) is under God's just condemnation. Breaking God's holy law incurs a just penalty (2:2), namely, eternal separation from God in hell. "The wages of sin is death" (Rom. 6:23). God's wrath abides on the one who does not obey Jesus Christ (John 3:36). As Jonathan Edwards pictured it in his famous sermon, "Sinners in the Hands of an Angry God," every sinner is like a spider dangling by a thread over a fire. Only God's mercy keeps us from falling into the eternal flames.

Salvation does not mean, as one late popular TV preacher put it, "to be changed from a negative to a positive self image" (Robert Schuller, *Self-Esteem: The New Reformation* [Word], p. 68). Salvation does not mean that Jesus helps you fulfill your dreams. Salvation is not about Jesus improving your marriage or giving you peace and joy. God's salvation isn't a nice thing to round out your otherwise successful and happy life. Salvation is about Jesus rescuing you from the wrath to come! And since every person is in imminent danger of facing that wrath, salvation is every person's greatest need!

> B. Salvation is great because it comes to us from none other than the Lord Jesus Himself.

"For this reason" (2:1) points back to chapter 1, where the author has extolled the supremacy of Jesus, God's eternal Son. He is God's final word to us, the heir of all things, and the creator of the universe. He is the radiance of God's glory and the exact representation of His nature. He upholds all things by the word of His power. He made purification for sins and now sits at the right hand of the Majesty on high (1:2-3). He is far superior to the angels, who worship and serve Him (1:4-14). "For *this* reason," because Jesus is the glorious Son of God who went to the cross to secure your purification from sin, your salvation is indescribably great.

> As I said, there is not a word of application in chapter 1. Rather, chapter 1 sets forth the doctrine of the exalted person of Jesus Christ in relation to the Father and to the angels. It is only after the author has set forth this doctrine that he gives this first exhortation. Sound doctrine must always be the foundation for practical application.

And yet we live in a day when many pastors are minimizing doctrine. I've heard things like, "Doctrine is divisive." Or, "People don't need theology or biblical content. They need to know how to get along in their marriages and how to deal with life's problems." So pastors are giving sermons (if you could even call them that!) that are devoid of doctrine. Frankly, many such sermons could easily appear in *Reader's Digest* without much modification!

But our author wants us to see the connection between the great doctrines about Christ in chapter 1 and his exhortation here: "For this reason…" (2:1). Our salvation is indescribably great because it comes to us from none other than the eternal Son of God who left the Majesty on high to become the sacrifice for our sins. He announced this good news during His earthly ministry (2:3). His teaching shows us the way to be reconciled to God. Having offered Himself for our sins and rising from the dead, He is now back at the right hand of God, awaiting the time when His enemies become His footstool (1:13). How can we escape if we neglect so great a salvation!

C. Salvation is great because eyewitnesses confirmed it as true.

Salvation is only great if it is true. If it's just someone's fanciful idea, with no factual basis, it may be nice, but it certainly isn't worth suffering the loss of your property or shedding your blood for (10:34; 12:4). This great salvation was not only "at the first spoken through the Lord," but also "it was confirmed to us by those who heard" (2:3). That statement seems to place the author, along with his readers, in the category of those who did not hear the gospel directly from Jesus Christ, which would exclude Paul from being the author. Those who hold to Pauline authorship say that this is just an editorial "us." But whoever he was, the point is the gospel that Jesus proclaimed comes to us from those who directly witnessed His earthly ministry.

The gospel is not the best ideas of a bunch of religious philosophers speculating about how they think we can be reconciled to God. The gospel is a matter of revelation and historical fact. Jesus really lived. His teaching and miracles are truthfully recorded in the gospels. He died on the cross and was raised physically from the grave before He ascended bodily into heaven. Many eyewitnesses saw these things and recorded them for us. If they were fictional stories, those in that day who read these accounts would have laughed the apostles out of town. But rather, these witnesses held to the truth about Jesus, even when cost them their lives.

D. Salvation is great because God Himself confirmed the message by miracles through the apostles.

God testifies through these witnesses "by signs and wonders and by various miracles and by gifts of the Holy Spirit according to His will" (2:4). He is referring to the miracles performed mostly by the apostles as recorded in the Book of Acts. The terms, "signs, wonders, and miracles" are basically synonymous, but have different nuances. *Signs* point to the fact that miracles have spiritual significance. When a lame man is healed or a dead man is raised, it points to something beyond the bare fact. These are pictures of how God powerfully acts to save souls. *Wonders* emphasize the human response of awe and amazement when we witness God doing the humanly impossible. *Various* (=

"manifold" or "many-colored") *miracles* (= Greek, *dynamis*) focus on God's power displayed in numerous ways.

Gifts [lit., distributions] *of the Holy Spirit* are given "according to His will." This emphasizes God's sovereignty in bestowing spiritual gifts as He sees fit for His purposes (1 Cor. 12:11). As Paul explains in 1 Corinthians 12, not everyone has the same gifts, but as in the human body, so in the body of Christ each member has a vital function for the overall health of the body.

Many claim that the church should receive and exercise the miraculous gifts (miracles, healings, speaking in tongues, interpretation of tongues, word of knowledge, and prophecy) to the same extent as the early church did. Others argue that such gifts entirely ceased with the close of the New Testament canon. It seems to me that those who emphasize such gifts overlook God's purpose for them. He gave these gifts to confirm the gospel. If you study miracles in the Bible, you will find that they are not uniformly distributed. They occur in clusters at critical times in history.

It would seem that these gifts had diminished by the time Hebrews was written. Otherwise the author would not have referred to the miracles done by the apostles. Rather he would have called attention to the ongoing phenomena in their midst, which would have strengthened his point. Even in Paul's ministry, there seems to be a chronological tapering off of such miracles. In Acts 19, even handkerchiefs carried from Paul to those who were sick brought healing. But at the end of his life, he didn't tell Timothy to claim healing for his stomach problems by faith, or to wait until the handkerchief arrived. He told him to drink a little wine (in modern terms, "take your medicine"; 1 Tim. 5:23). Paul didn't heal Trophimus, but left him sick at Miletus (2 Tim. 4:20).

So it would seem that these miraculous gifts are not God's normal way of operating in this era. But we should not restrict His ability to perform miracles if it is His sovereign will. With regard to speaking in tongues, Scripture clearly teaches that the genuine gift is miraculously speaking in an unlearned foreign language. It definitely is *not* jabbering in nonsense syllables! That fact alone eliminates about 99 percent of what goes under the guise of speaking in tongues in our day. Paul gives a number of other guidelines that should govern the practice of this gift, but which most charismatic churches ignore (1 Cor. 14:27-34).

To sum up the first point: because every person desperately needs salvation, because it comes to us from none other than God's exalted Son, because it was confirmed to us as true from those who were with Jesus, and because God confirmed their testimony through miracles, it is indescribably great.

2. Because God's salvation is so great, the consequences of neglecting it are terrible.

The author does not specify here what we will face if we neglect this salvation. But all we have to do is read ahead (10:27), where he gets more graphic: If we don't escape, we face "a terrifying expectation of judgment and the fury of a fire which will consume the adversaries" (see also 12:25-29). Perhaps you're thinking, "How can these frightening warnings apply to Christians? Aren't believers eternally secure?"

One of the mistaken ideas that the author of Hebrews confronts in this and in every other warning section is what we could call "the myth of the carnal Christian." This idea was popularized by Lewis Sperry Chafer's *He That is Spiritual* [Dunham] and by the *Schofield Reference Bible* (note on 1 Cor. 2:14) early in the 20th century. It was later picked up by Campus Crusade's booklet, "How to Be Filled with the Holy Spirit." The idea is that there are three classes of people: the natural man (unbeliever); the spiritual man (the Spirit-filled believer); and, the carnal man (the believer who is running his own life, not subject to the Holy Spirit). For the sake of time, I cannot go into many of the problems with this classification (see Ernest Reisinger's booklet, "What Should We Think of the Carnal Christian?" [Banner of Truth]).

But one problem is that it gives false assurance to the person who says, "I believe in Jesus as my Savior, so I am going to heaven. But I am not submitting to Him as my Lord." For the author of Hebrews, either you are holding fast to your confession of faith in Christ and are striving against sin, or you are drifting spiritually and are in danger of frightening judgment. Those are the *only* options.

True believers may drift and may get entangled in sin. But when they are confronted with the truth, they will turn from their sin and pursue holiness. If they do not turn from it, they have no basis for assurance of salvation. The longer they continue in sin, the more reason they have to question whether their profession of faith was genuine. But no one has the option of saying, "I'm just a carnal Christian. I'm living for this world now, but when I die I'll go to heaven." That option does not exist.

The author sets forth the consequences of neglecting salvation by contrasting the Law with the gospel.

A. The Law imposed some frightening penalties for disobedience.

"The word spoken by angels" refers to the Law given to Moses on Mount Sinai. The Old Testament does not state directly that angels gave the Law to Moses, but it implies such (Deut. 33:2; Ps. 68:17) and the New Testament confirms it (Acts 7:38, 53; Gal. 3:19). That Law imposed frightening penalties for sin. Any defiant disobedience was punished by stoning to death (Num. 15:30, 32-36; Josh. 7:1-26). Sometimes God sent punishment directly from heaven, such as when the ground opened and swallowed up Korah and his fellow rebels (Num. 16), or when God sent plagues among the people (Num. 16:46-50; 21:6-9; 25:8-9). In these judgments, God was not being cruel; He was acting in justice (Heb. 2:2).

B. The neglect of the gospel will bring far worse consequences.

The argument is from the lesser to the greater. Greater revelation imposes greater responsibility. If the Jews under the Law were punished for their disobedience, how much more will we come under God's judgment if we associate with God's people, but turn our backs on the great salvation that is offered through the death of God's own Son? That is his argument and appeal.

We err if we think that the demands of the gospel are less exacting than those of the Law. We also err if we think that grace means that we can be sloppy about God's standards of holiness, while He just shrugs His shoulders. That is a dangerously wrong way to think! As the author states (10:29), "How much severer punishment do you think he will deserve who has trampled under foot the Son of God, and has regarded as unclean the blood of the covenant by which he was sanctified, and has insulted the Spirit of grace?" To drift away from the gospel after you've been exposed to it is to turn away from God Himself, who sent His Son so that we could have His gift of salvation. You don't want to do that!

3. **In spite of the greatness of God's salvation, we all are in danger of drifting away from it.**

The Danger of Drifting Spiritually

As I said, the author uses "we" to include himself as vulnerable. The immediate cause of the Hebrews' drifting was that they were facing trials and the threat of persecution. Whenever we are there, we need to be on guard. We are then most in danger of drifting. But even at other times, drifting is easy because all it requires is neglect.

    A.   The cause of drifting is neglect.

Usually drifting is inadvertent. If you've ever steered a boat, you know that if you do not deliberately keep it on course, you will drift with the currents. The stronger the current, the more you have to give constant attention to keep the boat on course. Since we live in the strong current of this evil world, we all are prone to drift with the culture.

It does not take active rebellion or defiance against God to go to hell. Simple neglect of salvation while you attend to other things will do the trick nicely. The Greek word "pay attention" (2:1) is used in the parable Jesus told about the king who invited guests to his son's wedding party: "they paid no attention and went their way, one to his own farm, another to his business" (Matt. 22:5). There's nothing inherently sinful about farms and businesses—unless they cause you to neglect the king's invitation! Someone put it this way: "What must I do to be lost? Nothing!" Just drift through life, paying attention to other things.

    B.   The antidote to drifting is paying attention.

"We must pay much closer attention to what we have heard" (2:1). If you attend a church where God's great salvation is proclaimed from week to week, pay attention to the message! Don't tune it out and think about what you're going to do with your week. Don't yawn and think, "I wish the pastor would be more interesting." Pay attention to this great salvation!

Start with the basics: Are you giving deliberate effort to seeking God and His salvation? How much attention have you given to understand the gospel? Do you pore over Scripture as you would read a will if you thought a rich relative had left you an inheritance? Do you read and study God's Word as His treasure entrusted to your soul? Is spending time alone with God in His Word and prayer a priority in your schedule?

How much effort do you put into such a great salvation? Do you set some spiritual goals to help you grow? Do you look for solid books to read that will help you know God better? Do you listen to sermons from godly men that help you become more godly? Do you cut out of your life anything that would divert you from such a great salvation?

Conclusion

It's wonderful to fall in love and get married. I highly recommend the experience! But marriage is a relationship, and relationships take time and effort to maintain. I don't care how deeply you were in love when you got married, if you neglect your marriage and devote your attention to other things, your marriage will fail. Marriage is a wonderful gift from God and is worth the time and effort it takes to maintain and deepen that relationship.

But salvation is a far greater gift than marriage, because it has to do with our eternal destiny! Don't let it drift! Don't neglect it! Don't get distracted with other things, even with good things! Because our salvation is so great, we must pay closer attention to it, so that we don't drift away from it. *You are either drifting with regard to your salvation because of neglect, or you are growing because of deliberate effort and attention.* Which is it for you?

Application Questions

1. What are some practical ways to keep the greatness of salvation before you at all times?

2. Agree/disagree: A professing Christian who is in sin has no basis for assurance of salvation.

3. Should we seek miraculous sign gifts in our day? Give biblical support for your answer.

4. Some teach that the Christian life does not involve our effort. Does this view reflect the biblical balance? Why/why not?

Hebrews 2:5-9, New American Standard Bible 1995

5 For He did not subject to angels the world to come, concerning which we are speaking. 6 But one has testified somewhere, saying,

> "What is man, that You remember him?
> Or the son of man, that You are concerned about him?
> 7 "You have made him for a little while lower than the angels;
> You have crowned him with glory and honor,
> And have appointed him over the works of Your hands;
> 8 You have put all things in subjection under his feet."

For in subjecting all things to him, He left nothing that is not subject to him. But now we do not yet see all things subjected to him.

9 But we do see Him who was made for a little while lower than the angels, namely, Jesus, because of the suffering of death crowned with glory and honor, so that by the grace of God He might taste death for everyone.

Our Glorious Destiny in Christ
Hebrews 2:5-9

What would you do with a 19-year-old Christian young man, who wrote in his diary, "9. *Resolved,* To think much, on all occasions, of my dying, and of the common circumstances which attend death"? As you read through his 70 resolutions, you encounter things like, "7. *Resolved,* Never to do any thing, which I should be afraid to do if it were the last hour of my life." "17. *Resolved,* That I will live so, as I shall wish I had done when I come to die."

If that young man lived in a modern evangelical home, his parents would probably be looking for a good Christian psychologist to get this kid's focus off of such morbid subjects. Maybe an anti-depressant would help!

That young man was Jonathan Edwards, who went on to become the great revivalist preacher of the First Great Awakening (his resolutions are in *The Works of Jonathan Edwards* [Banner of Truth], 1:xx-xxi). His writings are still immensely helpful to believers, 300 years later. Lest you think that he was a gloomy, depressive type, I should point out that his first resolution was, in part, "1. *Resolved,* That *I will do whatsoever* I think to be most to the glory of God, and my own good, profit, and pleasure, in the whole of my duration; without any consideration of the time, whether now, or never so many myriads of ages hence." Edwards realized, even as a teenager, that to live for God's glory in light of death and eternity was to live for the greatest personal good, profit, and pleasure.

It seems to me that modern evangelical Christians are far too focused on the here and now. We've lost the central focus that Edwards had, even as a teenager, of living each day in view of death and eternity. The modern view is, "Heaven is a nice thought, but I want the good life *now*. If Jesus can help me succeed in my family, in business, and in my personal emotional life, *that's* what I want! I'll think about heaven when I'm in my eighties."

As a result of our shortsightedness, we don't handle trials well. It is unknown how we might handle persecution, should such arise against the American church, but it probably would free up a few seats on Sunday mornings. I agree with John Piper (in a message on Charles Simeon; www.desiringgod.org), who observed over a decade ago that evangelical pastors are too emotionally fragile. If we catch strong criticism or personal attacks, we're quick to bail out of the ministry. One main reason for this weakness is that we are not focused on our glorious eternal destiny in Jesus Christ.

A main practical theme of the Letter to the Hebrews is endurance under trials. The author frequently exhorts his readers (3:6; see also 3:14; 4:14; 6:11-12), "Hold fast our confidence and the boast of our hope firm until the end." Or (10:36), "For you have need of endurance, so that when you have done the will of God, you may receive what was promised."

In order to give his readers the perspective to endure, the author focuses on their eternal destiny in Christ. In 1:14, in his argument that Jesus is greater than the angels, he pointed out that the angels serve "those who will inherit salvation." While we now possess salvation (if we have trusted in Christ), much of it is reserved for eternity as our inheritance. As Paul puts it in Romans 8:17-18, we are now children of God, "and if children, heirs also, heirs of God and fellow-heirs with Christ, if indeed we suffer with Him in order that we may also be glorified with Him. For I consider that the sufferings of this present time are not worthy to be compared with the glory that is to be revealed to us." To endure our present sufferings, we must focus on the glory ahead in Christ.

That is the train of thought in Hebrews 2:5-9. After his brief exhortation to pay attention so that we do not drift (2:1-4), he comes back to deal with Jesus' superiority over the angels. It is difficult to say whether the opening word, "for," links back to 1:14 or to the entire preceding argument. It is likely that he was thinking of an objection that some of his Jewish readers who were wavering might have had. They may have been thinking, "If the Son of God is greater than the angels, having obtained a more excellent name than they (1:4), then how does this fit with His becoming a man, since men are lower than the angels? Furthermore, how does this fit with His dying on the cross, since angels never die? How then is Jesus superior to the angels?"

The author responds by showing that God did not subject the world to come to angels, but to man. To support this point, he cites from Psalm 8 (LXX). His introduction of the quote, "one has testified somewhere," does not mean that he couldn't remember where the quote was from. He cites it accurately (the original probably omits the last part of 2:7, "and have appointed him over the works of Your hands"). Rather, the author wants to emphasize that the quote comes from God, rather than to draw attention to David, the human author. Psalm 8 reflects on the high position to which God appointed man, putting him over all creation.

But, the author adds (2:8), "we do not yet see all things subjected to him." The unstated but obvious event that overturned man's high position was the fall. Then, in verse 9, he shows that Jesus (the first use of His name in the book, obviously emphasizing His humanity), because of His death on our behalf, was crowned with glory and honor. Thus He recovered what man lost in the fall. In the world to come, redeemed man will reign with Jesus as God intended. So the main idea is that…

Although God's original high purpose for man was lost in the fall, it will be recovered through Jesus Christ.

Because the train of thought is not easy here, I need to explain the text first. Then I will apply it.

1. God's original intent for man was that we rule over the earth (2:5-8a).

He makes two points here:

A. Man's destiny is higher than that of the angels (2:5).

"For He did not subject to angels the world to come, concerning which we are speaking." There is debate about the meaning of the phrase, "the world to come." The Greek word for "world" means "the inhabited earth." Some take the whole phrase to refer to the messianic age inaugurated by Christ at His first coming. Others understand it to refer to the future Millennial Kingdom.

In the original creation, God created man in His image to subdue the earth and rule over it (Gen. 1:26-28). Man lost that dominion to Satan in the fall, so that he is now "the ruler of this world" (John 12:31; 14:30; 16:11; also, 2 Cor. 4:4; Eph. 2:2; 6:12; 1 John 5:19). At the cross, Jesus overcame Satan's power (John 12:31; 16:11). Christ's victory will be finalized in His second coming and kingdom rule. At the end of that 1,000-year kingdom, Satan will be loosed briefly for one final assault on Christ's kingdom, only to be defeated and judged forever (Rev. 20:7-10).

Thus I understand "the world to come" to refer primarily to the future Millennial Kingdom. But there is currently a heavenly conflict for dominion on earth. We participate in this conflict and reign with Christ as we conquer the strongholds of Satan through spiritual warfare (Eph. 6:10-20; Dan. 10). To the extent that we live under Christ's lordship, we experience a taste of His kingdom rule now. But the full expression of Christ's kingdom awaits His return, when He will reign over all the earth. Then we will reign with Him, and we will judge the angels (1 Cor. 6:3). So our ultimate destiny is higher than that of the angels, since we will rule the world to come with Christ.

B. God's original intent for us is described in Psalm 8 (2:6-8).

David was probably standing out under the night sky, gazing at the impressive array of stars, when he marveled, "O Lord, our Lord, how majestic is Your name in all the earth, who have displayed Your splendor above the heavens!" As he considers his own smallness in light of the immensity of the universe, he marvels, "What is man, that You remember him, or the son of man that You are concerned about him?" David stands amazed as he realizes that, in spite of man's insignificance compared to the vast universe, God has appointed man below the angels to rule over creation.

The phrase, "a little lower than the angels," is ambiguous. It can mean either "by a small degree" or "for a short time." The former sense fits the psalm as applied to man, who lacks the supernatural powers of the angels. The latter sense fits the psalm as applied to the Son of Man, who laid aside His glory for a short time to take on human flesh while on this earth (Philip E. Hughes, *A Commentary on the Epistle to the Hebrews* [Eerdmans], p. 85). He retains His humanity forever, but when He ascended, He took back His glory (John 17:5; Rev. 1:12-18).

As the Psalm unfolds, God created man as the apex of His creation, giving him great glory and honor. He gave man a position of authority, to rule over all other creatures. Adam and Eve were in a perfect environment, enjoying perfect fellowship with their Creator. Man's original high position of honor shows how utterly inexcusable the fall was! What more could Adam and Eve have wanted? What did they lack? They had position, prestige, and power over everything on earth! Yet, they wanted more, to be like God Himself.

After citing the line of the Psalm, "You have put all things in subjection to his feet," the author of Hebrews explains (2:8), "For in subjecting all things to him, He left nothing that is not subject to him. But now we do not yet see all things subjected to him." The question is, does "him" refer to man or to Christ? It probably refers to man in the first place, but also beyond man to Christ as the representative Man (F. F. Bruce, *Commentary on the Epistle to the Hebrews* [Eerdmans], p. 37). As Bruce explains (*ibid.*), "The writer confesses that it is not easy to recognize in man the being whom the psalmist describes as 'crowned with glory and honor' and enjoying dominion over all the works of the Creator's hands." But, as he will explain in verse 9, man's failed purpose is fulfilled in Christ. The author refers to that failed purpose in 2:8b:

2. God's original intent for man was hindered by our fall into sin (2:8b).

The fall looms behind the words, "But we do not yet see all things subjected to him." The author, then, is saying that Psalm 8 had reference to the first Adam, created in God's image to have dominion over His creation. Everything without exception was to be subject to man. That was God's original intent, but that is not what we now see. Man fell through sin, thus thwarting the fulfillment of everything in creation being subject to him.

> As a result of the fall, God ordained that the earth would be cursed, so that man would have to till it by the sweat of his brow (Gen. 3:17-19). Adam and Eve were expelled from the garden, losing their place of dominion. The human race became subject to sickness, injury, and death. The effects of sin infected the entire race, so that Adam and Eve's first son murdered his brother. Man became subject to what we call "natural disasters," such as earthquakes, volcanoes, floods, fires, tornadoes, hurricanes, drought, and extremes of heat and cold.

John MacArthur describes it this way (*The MacArthur New Testament Commentary, Hebrews* [Moody], p. 57):

> Man lives in jeopardy every hour. Just at the height of professional achievement, his brain may develop a tumor, and he becomes an imbecile. Just at the brink of athletic fame, he may be injured and become a helpless paralytic. He fights himself, he fights his fellowman, and he fights his earth. Every day we read and hear of the distress of nations, of the

impossibility of agreement between statesmen in a world that languishes in political and social conflict—not to mention economic hardship, health hazards, and military threats. We hear the whine of pain from dumb animals and even see the struggle of trees and crops against disease and insects. Our many hospitals, doctors, medicines, pesticides, insurance companies, fire and police departments, funeral homes—all bear testimony to the cursed earth.

Even if we look beyond man as the reference in 2:8b, to Christ as the representative Man, we do not yet see all things subjected to Him. That idea ties back to 1:13, where the Father says to the Son, "Sit at My right hand, until I make Your enemies a footstool for Your feet." That has not yet happened. In God's sovereign plan, He allows wicked men and nations to rage against His Messiah in this present age. But the day is coming when He "shall break them with a rod of iron" and "shatter them like earthenware" (Ps. 2:9). This leads to the third link in the author's thought:

3. God's original intent for man will be realized through Jesus Christ (2:9).

The order of thought here follows Paul's treatment of Jesus' humiliation and glory in Philippians 2:5-11. There, Jesus who existed in the form of God emptied Himself of His glory, took on the form of a servant, and became obedient to death on a cross. Therefore, God highly exalted Him and bestowed on Him the name that is above every name.

Here, Jesus, the eternal Son of God (Hebrews 1) humbled Himself by taking on human flesh, becoming "a little lower than the angels." But He didn't stop there. He submitted to "the suffering of death," "so that by the grace of God He might taste death for everyone." As a result, He is now "crowned with glory and honor." To "taste death" means not to nibble at it but, rather, to experience death to the fullest degree. "Everyone" refers to all that will experience the benefits of Christ's death through faith, the "many sons" whom He will bring to glory (2:10).

The risen Jesus chided the two men on the Emmaus Road for not believing in all that the prophets had spoken. Then He said, "Was it not necessary for the Christ to suffer these things and to enter into His glory?" (Luke 24:26).

Peter said that the prophets sought "to know what person or time the Spirit of Christ within them was indicating as He predicted the sufferings of Christ and the glories to follow" (1 Pet. 1:11). In other words, Jesus' death was not unforeseen. The Old Testament prophets had predicted His death and after it, His glory.

This was God's ordained means of rescuing the fallen human race from the ravages of sin and restoring us to the place of His original intention. If we are in Christ through faith, then we are seated in the heavenly places in Him. If He is now crowned with glory and honor, then we share that glory and honor, although we do not yet see it (Heb. 2:7; Ps. 8:5). When He comes again to reign in His kingdom, we will reign with Him! That is our glorious destiny in Christ!

To recap, Christ's incarnation and death did not in any way imply His inferiority to angels. This is supported by the fact that God ordained that man will rule angels in the world to come. Psalm 8 shows that this was God's original intent. That intent was hindered by the fall, but now has been recovered in the second Adam, the Lord Jesus Christ. Through His death, resurrection, exaltation on high, and coming again to reign, we will reign with Him.

Conclusion

Hopefully, you now understand the flow of thought in this text. How should we apply these verses practically?

First, we should not let present trials cause us to neglect our great salvation, because one day we shall reign with Christ. A. W. Pink (*An Exposition of Hebrews* [electronic ed.], Ephesians Four Group: Escondido, CA, p. 97) said, "The *practical* bearings of this verse on the Hebrews was: Continue to hold fast your allegiance to Christ, for the time is coming when those who do so shall enter into a glory surpassing that of the angels." In other words, we need to develop and maintain the eternal perspective of our glorious destiny in Christ so that we can endure joyfully our present trials. If Jesus had to suffer first and then enter His glory, so do we. God used suffering to perfect His Son (2:10), and He does so with us. Jonathan Edwards was right: we should focus often on the shortness of life in light of eternity.

Victoria was Queen of England from 1837 to 1901. When she was young, she was shielded from the fact that she would be the next ruling monarch of

England, lest this knowledge should spoil her. When her teacher finally let her discover that she would one day be Queen of England, Victoria's response was, "Then I will be good." Her life would be controlled by her future destiny.

Our situation should parallel hers. Our future destiny is that we will reign with Jesus Christ, not for a few years, but throughout eternity. Our knowledge of that should enable us to endure present hardships and trials. We should live as set apart unto Christ because we look ahead to our glorious destiny.

Second, by faith we should see Jesus and marvel at what He did for us and that we are now in Him (2:9). He left the splendor of heaven and not only took on human flesh, but also went to the cross on our behalf! "Amazing love, how can it be, that Thou, my God, shouldst die for me?" (Charles Wesley). That is why our Lord ordained Communion, so that we would remember Him and what He did on the cross for us. Paul said, "I have been crucified with Christ; and it is no longer I who live, but Christ lives in me; and the life which I now live in the flesh I live by faith in the Son of God, who loved me, and delivered Himself up for me" (Gal. 2:20). Paul daily saw Jesus, who endured the cross on his behalf. And, he saw himself in Christ, so that all the benefits of Christ's death applied to him. That is how we should live each day.

Third, if you feel weak, despised, or insignificant in this evil world, take courage! In Christ, we are more than conquerors. Although it is difficult to fathom, in the ages to come we will reign with Christ in His kingdom. It doesn't really matter what the world thinks of you. What matters is what God thinks of you. If you have trusted Christ as the One who bore your sins on the cross, then God has imputed His righteousness to you. You are purified from your sins. You can know that although you are just a speck on planet earth, which is just a speck in this gigantic universe, God cares for you and has a purpose for your life. That purpose transcends the short life we have in this body and extends through eternity in our glorified bodies that we will receive when Christ returns.

But there is a final truth that may apply to some: *If you are not in Christ, you should greatly fear.* Though He is now despised and ignored by millions around the world, the day is coming when they will cry out for the rocks to fall on them and hide them from the presence of Him who sits on the throne, and from the wrath of the Lamb (Rev. 6:16). He is that chief cornerstone, which the builders rejected. If you build your life on Him, you will find a sure foundation for every storm in life (Matt. 7:24-25). But if that Stone falls on you, it will scatter you like dust (Matt. 21:44). "Do homage to the Son, that He not become angry, and you perish in the way, for His wrath may soon be kindled. How blessed are all who take refuge in Him" (Ps. 2:12).

Application Questions

1. How, practically, can we keep our focus on our eternal destiny in the midst of life's problems?

2. Sometimes Psalm 8 is used to teach the unbiblical concept of "self-esteem." Was David's response to these truths to glorify himself or God? Is it proper to have a sense of significance as those created in God's image?

3. To what extent do the effects of the fall remain in believers? To what extent are these effects removed?

4. Is the Christian life just "pie in the sky when you die"? To what extent should we experience the abundant life now? What exactly does that mean?

Hebrews 2:10, New American Standard Bible 1995

10 For it was fitting for Him, for whom are all things, and through whom are all things, in bringing many sons to glory, to perfect the author of their salvation through sufferings.

Why Jesus' Death Was Fitting
Hebrews 2:10

Although there are many that oppose capital punishment, when a notoriously evil person, such as a terrorist or mass murderer, dies, most of us would say, "It was fitting that he die." After all, he was responsible for the deaths of many innocent people. Capital punishment serves justice and warns those who may consider committing a similar crime that they will be executed. And so we can rightly say, "It was fitting for that despicable man to die."

But we would be shocked if someone whose father had died of natural causes said, "It was fitting for him to die." Or, consider a good man who never did anything to hurt others. To the contrary, he did many good deeds to help those in need, even at great personal cost. He always took kind interest in those whom society rejected. He had a special love for children. He labored to the point of exhaustion in serving others. If *this* kind of man were executed, how could anyone say, "It was fitting that he die?"

But that is precisely what the author of Hebrews says about the death of Jesus Christ. He says that it was fitting for God to put His own Son to death (2:10). This verse must have jarred his Jewish Christian readers! They were struggling with the offense of the cross. Although they had believed in Jesus, they were being tempted by unbelieving Jews who said, "How could Jesus be the Messiah if He died? Our Messiah will conquer all our enemies, not die. Your Messiah didn't die a heroic death or even a normal death. Rather, He died as a common criminal, in the most shameful death imaginable, on a Roman cross! You want us to believe that this Man is our Savior? You've got to be kidding!"

So the author is showing why Jesus' death did not disqualify Him as Messiah and Savior. It did not mean that He was inferior to the angels, who do not die. In fact, Jesus' death was God's very means not only to glorify Jesus, but also to bring many sons to glory. It was part of God's eternal plan. So the author wants to remove the offense of the cross for his readers so that they will not be ashamed to proclaim it as the very power and wisdom of God (1 Cor. 1:23-24) and to rejoice in it. Our text shows that...

Why Jesus' Death Was Fitting

It was fitting for Jesus to die in order to effect our salvation in line with God's eternal plan and His perfect attributes.

Before I started studying this passage, I had planned to cover verses 10-18 in one chapter. After I dug into it, I shortened it to verses 10-13. But further study made me think, "There's more than enough in verse 10 alone for one chapter!" The author gives us five reasons why it was fitting for Jesus to die. I hope to deepen our understanding of the glory of the cross of Christ.

1. Jesus' death was fitting because it works for God's glory in accord with His eternal purpose.

The author could have just referred to God as God. Why does he here add, "for whom are all things, and through whom are all things"? Leon Morris explains (*Expositor's Bible Commentary*, ed. by Frank Gaebelein [Zondervan], 12:26), "The words show that the sufferings of Jesus did not take place by chance. They have their place in God's great eternal purpose." The cross did not thwart God's plan; it fulfilled it.

Peter emphasized this same truth in his sermon on the Day of Pentecost (Acts 2:23): "This Man, delivered over by the predetermined plan and foreknowledge of God, you nailed to a cross by the hands of godless men and put Him to death." God's foreknowledge does not mean simply that God knew in advance what wicked men would do, and passively endorsed their behavior as His plan. Rather, in His eternal purpose God the Father determined to put His Son to death, and yet He is not responsible for the sin of those that did the horrible deed.

This truth is important enough that Luke saw fit to repeat it again in Acts 4:27-28, where in response to the threat of persecution, the early church prayed, "For truly in this city there were gathered together against Your holy servant Jesus, whom You anointed, both Herod and Pontius Pilate, along with the Gentiles and the peoples of Israel, to do whatever Your hand and Your purpose predestined to occur." The cross did not catch God or Jesus off guard. To the contrary, it was the very reason that He came to earth. In John 12:27 He said, "Now My soul has become troubled; and what shall I say, 'Father, save Me from this hour'? But for this purpose I came to this hour."

When I say that the cross works for God's glory, I mean that it displays the splendor and majesty of God's perfect attributes more than anything else in the universe. Glory is a somewhat elusive word to define. The Hebrew word has a root meaning of "heaviness," and thus of inherent worth or excellence. In the Bible, God's glory is often portrayed by a bright light, the *Shekinah*. Thus His glory is the outward, visible manifestation of His inward excellence and infinite worth.

Jonathan Edwards, in his treatise, "The End for Which God Created the World," gives a four-fold definition of glory (in John Piper, *God's Passion for His Glory* [Crossway Books], pp. 231-239). First, it denotes a person's internal excellence or greatness. Second, it refers to the exhibition of the internal glory, often seen as brightness in the case of God. Third, God's glory is the honor that we, as creatures, accord Him because He has imparted a knowledge of His excellence to us. Fourth, God's glory is the praise that we give Him. The third point emphasizes our *perception* of God's excellence, whereas this point emphasizes our *proclaiming* it.

When the author says that all things are *for* God and *through* God, he means that *God is the first and final cause of all that is* (see Piper, p. 184). Colossians 1:16 proclaims of Christ, "For by Him all things were created, both in the heavens and on earth, visible and invisible, whether thrones or dominions or rulers or authorities—all things have been created through Him and for Him." In Romans 11:36, Paul exults, "For from Him and through Him and to Him are all things. To Him be the glory forever. Amen." (See also, Proverbs 16:4.)

While we must never say that God is the author of evil (1 John 1:5; Hab. 1:13), we must not fall into the error of saying that evil is somehow not under God's sovereign decree or that evil operates outside of God's sovereign control. As we have already seen, the worst evil ever committed in the history of the world, the crucifixion of Jesus, was predetermined by God, and yet those who did it are fully responsible. While our finite brains cannot reconcile these things logically, we must accept them as God's revealed truth.

Also, the phrases, "for whom are all things, and through whom are all things," teach us that *God actively governs His creation*. Nothing can happen apart from His governance. He is working "all things after the counsel of His will" (Eph. 1:11). As the humbled King Nebuchadnezzar put it (Dan. 4:35), "He does according to His will in the host of heaven and among the inhabitants of earth; and no one can ward off His hand or say to Him, 'What have You done?'"

A. W. Pink wrote (*An Exposition of Hebrews* (electronic ed., 2000), Ephesians Four Group: Escondido, CA, p. 112),

> To believe and affirm that "for Him are all things, and by Him are all things" is simply owning that He is God—high above all, supreme over all, directing all. Anything short of this is, really, atheism.

And yet there are many Christians who deny that God is sovereign in salvation. They claim that to affirm this is to deny our "free will" and turn people into robots or puppets. Asahel Nettleton, a preacher whom God used in the Second Great Awakening to bring thousands to Christ, has a sermon on Psalm 97:1, "The Lord reigns, let the earth rejoice" (*Asahel Nettleton: Sermons from the Second Great Awakening* [International Outreach], pp.371-376). He raised the objection against the doctrine of election, that it robs people of free will. Then he said (372-373),

> We will drop the doctrine of decrees—How is it then? Does God operate on the hearts of men, or does he not? If not, then we must not pray that he would do it.
>
> No person can pray for himself without admitting that God can operate on his heart, and yet he be free.... [He then cites several verses that ask God to change our hearts.] But persons ought not to have prayed in this manner, if God could not answer their prayers without destroying their free agency. Ought we to pray that God would destroy our freedom?—that he would make us machines? This no one will pretend. How then can we pray that God would work in us that which is well pleasing in his sight, if as the objection supposes, he cannot operate on our hearts without destroying our freedom? ...
>
> It is a doctrine clearly taught in the scriptures, that a change of heart is absolutely necessary to prepare sinners for heaven. "Except a man be born again he cannot see the kingdom of God." We are also taught that God is the author of this change. "Born, not of blood, nor of the will of the flesh, nor of the will of man, but of God." But if God cannot operate

on the hearts of men without destroying their freedom, then we ought not to pray that God would renew the hearts of sinners. Surely we ought not to pray that God would convert men into machines. However wicked mankind may be, we cannot pray that God would stop them in their career of sin, because he cannot do it without destroying their freedom. When sinners have proud stubborn and rebellious hearts, we cannot pray that God would make them humble, submissive and obedient; because he cannot do it without converting them into machines.

He goes on to ask the question, "does God govern all his creatures and all their actions? Does he govern the actions of wicked men and devils?" He shows that God not only does this—without removing the freedom of sinners and without becoming the author of evil—but that this is a desirable thing, and a cause for rejoicing. Because if God does not govern all creatures, then we are in a very desperate situation.

Thus it was fitting for God to put Jesus to death, because it works for His glory in accord with His eternal purpose.

2. Jesus' death was fitting because it displays God's perfect attributes.

Have you ever heard someone say, "Why can't God just forgive sins without the cross? Why does He need to have blood shed in order to forgive? If someone wrongs me, I don't demand blood to be shed in order to forgive. Why can't God do that?"

The person saying that does not understand God's attributes. If God forgave sins without the shedding of blood, it would compromise His perfect righteousness and justice. Justice demands that the penalty for sin must be paid. On a human level, if a man broke into your parents' home and murdered your mother so that he could steal a few dollars for drug money, you would be outraged if the judge said, "We all make mistakes. Let's just let it go." That is not justice! So Jesus' death was befitting to the character of God.

Consider this a bit further. It befit God's **righteousness and holiness** to put His Son on the cross. God never winks at sin or lowers His standard of holiness. He hates sin so much that every wicked thought must be judged. All of the sins of God's elect were put upon His Son, so that it could be said (2 Cor. 5:21), "[God] made Him who knew no sin to be sin on our behalf, so that we might become the righteousness of God in Him." God's forgiveness never means that He just shrugs it off. Forgiveness means that Jesus bore God's awful wrath that I should have borne.

Also, the cross befit God's **power** (1 Cor. 1:24). The wrath of God is described as the lake of fire burns forever and ever without exhausting His wrath (Rev. 20:10-15). Jesus bore that wrath not on behalf of just one person, or a small group, but on behalf of the many sons that He would lead to glory! All of the sins of all of God's people for all time were piled on Jesus for those three hours of darkness on the cross, and yet, by God's strength, He endured!

Also, it befit God's **wisdom** (1 Cor. 1:24). How could God uphold His holiness and the just demands of the law, and yet be merciful to sinners? As Paul shows in Romans 3:21-26, the cross allows God to be both just and the justifier of the one who has faith in Jesus.

But the cross also befit God's **love and grace**. "God so loved the world, that He gave His only begotten Son, that whoever believes in Him shall not perish, but have eternal life" (John 3:16). F. F. Bruce (*Commentary on the Epistle to the Hebrews* [Eerdmans], p. 43) wrote, " It is in the passion of our Lord that we see the very heart of God laid bare; nowhere is God more fully or more worthily revealed as God than when we see Him 'in Christ reconciling the world unto himself' (2 Cor. 5:19)." "In this is love, not that we loved God, but that He loved us and sent His Son to be the propitiation for our sins" (1 John 4:10). As Charles Wesley wrote, "Amazing love, how can it be, that Thou my God shouldst die for me!"

Thus Jesus' death was fitting because it works for God's glory in accord with His eternal purpose, and because it upholds God's perfect attributes.

3. Jesus' death was fitting because it confirms His perfect humanity.

God perfected the author of our salvation through suffering. What does that mean? Wasn't Jesus already perfect? Yes, He is perfect in His divine attributes and He is perfect in His moral obedience. But to be qualified as the *Captain* or Leader of our salvation, He had to experience the suffering that humans go through as a result of the fall. To be our perfect *substitute*, He had to be without sin Himself, but He had to experience life as a human in this fallen world. To be our perfect *sympathetic high priest*, He had to be tempted in all things as we are, yet without sin (4:15).

I will deal with this more when we get to 2:18 and 4:15, but when we talk about Jesus being tempted, we must be careful not to project the pattern of our temptations onto Jesus. When we are tempted we are carried away and enticed by our own lusts (James 1:14). But Jesus did not have a sin nature as we do. In His humanity, He was like Adam and Eve *before* the fall. The trials that Jesus endured were real temptations in the sense that He experienced enticement from Satan to disobey God (Matt. 4:1-11). (The question of whether or not Jesus *could have sinned* will have to wait until Hebrews 4. My brief answer is, No!) But, He experientially learned obedience through the things that He suffered (Heb. 5:8). His suffering and death confirmed His perfect humanity and qualified Him as the Captain of our salvation.

4. Jesus' death was fitting because it confirms Him as the Captain of our salvation.

The word translated "author" (NASB) is used only four times in the New Testament, every time with regard to Jesus (Acts 3:15; 5:31; Heb. 12:2). It is one of more than 300 titles given to Jesus in Scripture (Pink, p. 112). It refers to one who "himself first takes part in that which he establishes" (B. F. Westcott, *The Epistle to the Hebrews* [Eerdmans], p. 49). Thus it can be translated "Captain," "Leader," or "Pioneer." Jesus blazed the trail of salvation before us (Bruce, p. 43). As the captain, He did not stay in the rear of the battle, giving orders to His troops on the front lines. Rather, He led the troops out in front, giving us the example to follow. Like Joshua leading Israel into the Promised Land, Jesus goes before His people, leading them to salvation.

John Owen (*An Exposition of Hebrews* [The National Foundation for Christian Education], 3:387-388) pointed out that Jesus went before us in three ways. He went before us *in obedience*, completely obeying and fulfilling God's holy law. He went before us *in suffering*, leaving us an example to follow in His steps (1 Pet. 2:21). And, He went before us *into glory*. Through His resurrection He has shown us that death is a defeated foe. Because He went through suffering into glory, He will take His people through the same course. He is leading many sons to glory.

Why Jesus' Death Was Fitting

5. **Jesus' death was fitting because it results in God's bringing many sons to glory.**

"Many" emphasizes the great number of the redeemed. Critics of the doctrine of election falsely accuse those who hold to it of believing that only a "select few" will be saved. But the Bible says no such thing! Charles Spurgeon and B. B. Warfield, who both vigorously defended the doctrine of election, also believed that the number of the saved will be greater than the number of the damned (see *C. H. Spurgeon Autobiography* [Banner of Truth], 1:171; and B. B. Warfield, *Biblical and Theological Studies* [P & R], pp. 334-350). Jonathan Edwards wrote, "As *much fruit* is the *glory* of the seed, so is the multitude of redeemed ones, which should spring from his death, his glory" (in Piper, p. 236, italics in original).

Jesus prayed that we might be with Him to see His glory (John 17:24). Paul said (Col. 3:4), "When Christ, who is our life, is revealed, then you also will be revealed with Him in glory." What does it mean to be brought to glory? This side of heaven no one can say for sure. It means, at the very least, that we will have glorious resurrection bodies, free from sin, sickness, infirmities, and death. It means that we will have a glorious purpose, to be with Christ and to praise and serve Him throughout eternity. "We will be like Him, because we will see Him just as He is" (1 John 3:3).

We can be assured that the Father will succeed in bringing many sons to glory, because it is *His* work that gets us there. The word "bring" is used in Luke 10:34 of the Good Samaritan, who brought the wounded man to an inn and took care of him. The man was too weak and wounded to bring himself there. The Samaritan did for him what he could not do for himself. "He who began a good work in you will perfect it until the day of Christ Jesus" (Phil. 1:6). Since salvation is God's work, secured for His people by the death and resurrection of His Son, He will succeed in spite of the onslaughts of the world, the flesh, and the devil against His sons and daughters.

Conclusion

I like the way John Calvin expressed it (*The Institutes of the Christian Religion* [Westminster], 2:1362):

This is the wonderful exchange which, out of his measureless benevolence, he has made with us; that, becoming Son of man with us, he has made us sons of God with him; that, by his descent to earth, he has prepared an ascent to heaven for us; that, by taking on our mortality, he has conferred his immortality upon us; that, accepting our weakness, he has strengthened us by his power; that, receiving our poverty unto himself, he has transferred his wealth to us; that, taking the weight of our iniquity upon himself (which oppressed us), he has clothed us with his righteousness.

Have you experienced this wonderful exchange personally? It is available to all who will come to the cross of Christ. Let go of the filthy rags of your own righteousness. Confess to God that you are a sinner deserving His wrath. Trust in the death of Jesus as the only acceptable payment for your sins. Then the cross will not be a stumbling block or foolishness to you, but rather the power and wisdom of God (1 Cor. 1:23-24). You will boast only in the cross (Gal. 6:14).

Application Questions

1. Why is the blood of Christ essential to our salvation? Why couldn't God just forgive us apart from the cross?

2. How could meditating often on the cross strengthen your walk with God?

3. How would you respond to a critic who asked, "Does God govern a world that includes child molesters and evil murderers? If He does, He is not good"?

4. In what sense was Jesus perfected through suffering? In what sense did He not need to be perfected?

Hebrews 2:11-15, New American Standard Bible 1995

11 For both He who sanctifies and those who are sanctified are all from one Father; for which reason He is not ashamed to call them brethren, 12 saying,

> "I will proclaim Your name to My brethren,
> In the midst of the congregation I will sing Your praise."

13 And again,

> "I will put My trust in Him."

And again,

> "Behold, I and the children whom God has given Me."

14 Therefore, since the children share in flesh and blood, He Himself likewise also partook of the same, that through death He might render powerless him who had the power of death, that is, the devil, 15 and might free those who through fear of death were subject to slavery all their lives.

Jesus Our Brother and Savior
Hebrews 2:11-15

Many years ago, I came to the realization that *ideas drive the world*. Karl Marx had some ideas about politics and the economy, called Communism, that held millions under its sway for the better part of the 20th century. Over a billion Chinese are still under that ideology. Quite often, the man in the street is unaware of the philosophic underpinnings for his behavior, but he is still very much influenced by certain prevailing philosophies and ideas.

For example, the teenager who dresses in black, mutilates his body, and listens constantly to rock music that exalts death, probably has not read any books on the philosophy of nihilism, but it controls his thought patterns and behavior. Millions of Americans could not articulate the philosophy of postmodernism, but it governs their daily lives. Wrong ideas can have devastating effects.

That is why I am committed to sound doctrine. Our ideas about God, man, sin, and salvation greatly affect the way we think, feel, act, and relate to one another. Sound doctrine produces healthy minds, hearts, and relationships. False doctrine results in wounded minds, hearts, and relationships.

Several years ago, I read a book titled *The Cruelty of Heresy* [Morehouse Publishing, 1993], by C. FitzSimons Allison, an Episcopalian bishop. In trying to communicate to his students the importance of the early church councils and creeds, Allison began asking the question, "What happens to someone who follows heretical teachings?" He says (p. 17), "It became quickly and readily apparent how cruel heretical teachings are and how prevalent the heresies are in contemporary times." Then he makes this astute observation (*ibid.*, italics his):

> We are susceptible to heretical teachings because, in one form or another, they nurture and reflect the *way we would have it be* rather than the *way God has provided*, which is infinitely better for us. As they lead us into the blind alleys of self-indulgence and escape from life, heresies pander to the most unworthy tendencies of the human heart. It is astonishing how little attention has been given to these two aspects of heresy: its cruelty and its pandering to sin.

The Letter to the Hebrews begins by spelling out the vital doctrine of the person of Jesus Christ. In chapter one, the author makes it clear that the Son of God is distinguished from the Father, and yet is fully God. Hebrews 1:3:

> He is the radiance of [God's] glory and the exact representation of His nature, and upholds all things by the word of His power. When He had made purification of sins, He sat down at the right hand of the Majesty on high.

He goes on to show that the Son of God is higher than the angels, whom He created and who worship and serve Him (1:4-14).

In chapter 2, after a brief exhortation, the author sets forth the truth that Jesus is also fully human. As the Cappadocians, a group of early church fathers, affirmed (Allison, p. 107, citing Gregory of Nyssa, *Against the Eunomians*, 2.10), "What he (Christ) did not assume he could not redeem.". To redeem people, Jesus had to assume human nature in its entirety, yet without sin.

In the early centuries of the church, there were several heresies regarding the person of Christ. All heresies contain *some* truth, but they emphasize those truths to the neglect of other biblical truths. The Docetic (from the Greek, *dokeo*, "to seem") heresy affirmed Jesus' deity, but denied His true humanity. They could not accept that, as God, Jesus really suffered. So they taught that He only *appeared* to suffer. A modern version of this heresy is Mary Baker Eddy's Christian Science cult, which teaches that suffering and even death are illusory and only exist because we lack faith (Allison, p. 30).

The Arian heresy denied Jesus' true deity, and declared that He was an intermediate deity, neither fully God nor fully man. Arius affirmed that Jesus was God's agent in creation, but he taught that Jesus was the first created being and was therefore subordinate to the Father. The Jehovah's Witnesses are modern Arians.

Apollinarius joined with Athanasius in fighting the Arians, but he went too far by asserting the unity of Christ's person as God, but at the expense of His true humanity. He did not go as far as the Docetists, in denying Jesus' physical existence or His suffering. But he limited Jesus' humanity to the physical, and taught that His soul and mind were divine only. Jesus had a human body, but His nature was not human, but divine. This is also called the Monophysite (= "one nature") heresy (Allison, pp. 107).

All of these imbalances were worked out at the Council of Chalcedon in 451, which affirmed that Christ is one person with two natures, the divine and the human, in unchangeable union. It maintained the unity of Christ's person, while distinguishing between His two natures, which are not confused or abolished because of the union (J. H. Hall, *Evangelical Dictionary of Theology*, ed. by Walter Elwell [Baker], p. 204).

All of this is background to our text, which affirms the humanity of Jesus. The author is showing that …

As the Captain of our salvation, Jesus became man in order to bring us to God.

The Puritans used to structure their sermons as "Doctrine" and "Use," which meant, "application." I think that their approach is helpful with this text, and so I follow it here:

The doctrine: Jesus became man to save us.

There are three points here:

1. As a man, Jesus' death secured our salvation (2:11a).

The word "for" directs us back to 2:10, where he said that God saw fit "to perfect the author of [our] salvation through sufferings." To save humans, Jesus had to assume full humanity. But, for His suffering and death to have merit before God, Jesus had to be fully God. In the incarnation, He did not lay aside His divinity, although He set aside His glory and He temporarily gave up the use of some of His divine attributes (omniscience, for example, John 11:34; Matt. 24:36). But He did fully assume our human nature.

In verse 11, Jesus is the one who sanctifies, which requires His being without sin. In Hebrews, the verb, "to sanctify," refers to the whole of salvation, not just to the aspect of progressive holiness (see 9:13; 10:10, 14, 29; 13:12). As Hebrews 10:10 puts it, "By this will we have been sanctified through the offering of the body of Jesus Christ once for all." F. F. Bruce explains (*Commentary on the Epistle to the Hebrews* [Eerdmans], p. 45),

By His death they are consecrated to God for His worship and service and set apart for God as His holy people, destined to enter into His glory. For sanctification is glory begun, and glory is sanctification completed.

Philip Hughes explains (*A Commentary on the Epistle to the Hebrews* [Eerdmans], p. 103),

> ... the "sanctification" of which our author speaks is intimately connected with and flows from Christ's priestly offering of himself on the cross. His consecration of himself is the source of our consecration (cf. Jn. 17:19).

The present tense participles in 2:11 "mark the continuous, personal application of Christ's work," both "in the individual soul and in the whole body of the Church" (B. F. Westcott, *The Epistle to the Hebrews* [Eerdmans], p. 50).

The author says, "both He who sanctifies and those who are sanctified are all from one" ("Father" has been added by the translators, but it is really an interpretation). Some (as the NASB) interpret this to refer to our common spiritual bond in God, but the context favors viewing it as a reference to our common human nature (see Hughes, pp. 104-105). The difference is that Jesus was holy and thus the sanctifier, whereas we are sinful and thus the object of His sanctification, which He accomplished on the cross. The main point is that Jesus had to assume our human nature fully in order to offer Himself as our substitute on the cross.

Before we leave this point, let me apply it briefly: *There is no such thing as salvation apart from sanctification.* It's all one package. When we get saved, we are set apart unto God. The actual working out of that holiness takes a lifetime, which invariably includes setbacks when we yield to sin. But the point is, every true believer is involved in the process of growing in sanctification, or holiness. As we're commanded in 12:14, we are to pursue "the sanctification, without which no one will see the Lord." It is *not optional* for believers to do battle against the flesh! Holiness is bound up with the very notion of salvation.

2. Jesus' humanity is so complete that He is not ashamed to call us brethren (2:11b-13).

Because Jesus took our humanity on Himself, He is not ashamed to call us brethren. In verse 14, it states that as God's children, we share in blood and flesh (literal order in Greek; it probably has no special significance; see Hughes,

p. 110, note 101). But Jesus "partook" of the same. Here a different verb and verb tense are used; the meaning is that the children naturally share in humanity (blood and flesh), but Jesus, at a fixed point in time, chose to partake of humanity (Bruce, p. 41, note 55). He existed eternally as God, but in the incarnation, He added a human nature and body to His deity, in order to redeem us. If Jesus were only a man, and not God, neither verse 11 nor 14 would make sense. Why would a man be ashamed to call fellow men "brothers"? Why would a man need to partake of human nature? Jesus' deity is assumed behind both verses.

The author goes on to support his point about Jesus' oneness with our humanity by quoting three Old Testament texts (from the Septuagint, the Greek translation), each of which makes a slightly different point.

A. As our brother, Jesus proclaims God's name to us (2:12).

Verse 12 quotes from Psalm 22:22. Psalm 22 is one of the most obviously messianic psalms in the Bible. It describes in detail a death by crucifixion centuries before that was known as a means of execution. Jesus cited Psalm 22:1 from the cross: "My God, My God, why have You forsaken Me?" The psalm goes on to describe the mocking of those who witnessed the crucifixion, the physical agony of the victim on the cross, and even the gambling for his clothes on the part of the soldiers. This section ends with the cry, "Save me from the lion's mouth," and the confident affirmation (Ps. 22:21), "From the horns of the wild oxen You answer me."

Then, the next verse is the one quoted in our text: "I will proclaim Your name to My brethren; in the midst of the congregation I will sing Your praise." There has been an obvious, radical change between verses 21 and 22, and we know that that change was the resurrection. God's name refers to His character and attributes, and here, especially, to His grace and mercy as seen in the cross. The word "brethren" in the first line of this verse is parallel to "congregation" in the second line, which is the Greek *ekklesia*, usually translated "church" in the New Testament. Jesus' brothers are the members of His church, those who are redeemed by His blood.

Two unrelated observations before we move on: First, *the fact that Jesus calls us His brethren should cause us to marvel and draw near to Him as One who understands our humanity*. But, we should refer to Jesus as our brother only in the most reverent and careful manner. While we should draw near in fellowship to Christ, we should never be too casual about our relationship with Him. Yes, we can marvel that He condescends to call us His brothers and sisters, but we must always remember that He is Lord. It would be as if you were a private in the army, and a general told you to call him by his first name. You may do that in certain situations, but on the base, around other soldiers, you should respect his office and always refer to him as the general. It would be arrogant for a private to be too chummy with the general. It would be a mark of humility for the general to call the private his brother.

Second, notice that *Jesus sings!* I don't often think of Him in that way, but here He says, "In the midst of the congregation I will sing Your praise." We know that after the Last Supper, Jesus and the disciples sang a hymn before they went out to the Mount of Olives (Matt. 26:30). If you want to know the words that they sang, you will find them in Psalms 115-118, the last part of the Hallel (they sang the first part, Psalms 113-114 before the Passover meal). We don't know the tunes! But if Jesus sang God's praise, and did it right before He went to the cross, as His people we, too, should sing God's praises, even when we face trials.

    B. As our brother, Jesus shows us practically how to trust God in the midst of trials (2:13a).

The second quote probably comes from the LXX of Isaiah 8:17 (it could be from 2 Sam. 22:3), with the third coming from Isaiah 8:18. This is a messianic section of Isaiah. Isaiah 7:14 is the familiar prophecy of the virgin bringing forth a son whose name would be Immanuel. In 8:14, it mentions that the Lord would become to Israel "stone to strike and a rock to stumble over" (see Rom. 9:33; 1 Pet. 2:8). In 9:6 is the well-known prophecy, "For a child will be born to us, a son will be given to us; and the government will rest on His shoulders; and His name will be called Wonderful Counselor, Mighty God, Eternal Father, Prince of Peace."

The point of this quote, where Messiah says that He puts His trust in God," is that in His humanity, Jesus depended on the Father for all things (John 5:19; 14:10). We see this supremely in His prayer life, since prayer is an expression of our complete dependence on God. As a man, Jesus demonstrated for us how we are to live, taking everything to God in prayer, trusting God for His sustenance and strength in every situation.

    C. As our brother, Jesus is the Son of God, and we are the children of God (2:13b).

Even though the quotes come from successive verses in Isaiah, the author adds, "And again," because he is making a different point. This quote may place Jesus in the role of Father (not brother), with the church as His children. Or, if Jesus is still viewed as our brother, then He is speaking as God's Son, thanking the Father for the spiritual children that the Father has given to Him, who are thus His brothers and sisters. Jesus is uniquely God's Son by eternal generation. We are God's children by the new birth, which God bestows on us through Christ (John 1:12). Either way, the point of the quote is that Jesus is identified with those He came to save. In John 6:37, Jesus refers to those who come to Him as those whom the Father gave to Him. Here, He calls us His children, whom God has given Him (John 13:33; 21:5). We can be sure that Jesus will not lose any of the children that the Father gives to Him (John 6:39). We are more precious to Him than any earthly father's children are to him, because Jesus gave His life so that we could join His family!

The first doctrinal point is that Jesus' death secured our sanctification. Second, Jesus' humanity is so complete that He is not ashamed to call us brethren. Finally,

3. Jesus' humanity and victory over death frees us from the power and fear of death (2:14-15).

This section goes through verses 16-18, which we'll look at in the following chapter. The fact of the incarnation is emphatically stated here, along with its purpose, "that through death, [Jesus] might render powerless him who had the power of death, that is, the devil, and might free those who through fear of death were subject to slavery all their lives." The bodily resurrection of Jesus is implicit behind these verses. If He had remained in the grave, He could not have rendered the devil powerless, nor could He have freed us from the power and fear of death. Those statements assume His victory over death through His resurrection.

Satan is described as the one who had the power of death. This does not mean that he has the power to kill people at will. The risen Christ holds the keys of death and Hades (Rev. 1:17, 18). God determines the length of each person's life (Ps. 139:16) and He alone has final authority in this matter (Job 2:6; Luke 12:5). But Satan tempted Adam and Eve to sin, and through sin, death entered this world. Satan was a murderer from the beginning (John 8:44). He delights in seeing people die outside of Christ, because they then join him in hell throughout eternity, which is the second death (Rev. 20:14-15).

Through His death and resurrection, Jesus paid the penalty of spiritual death that we had incurred through sin. Thus He delivers us from Satan's domain of darkness (Col. 1:13). Though believers still die physically, spiritually they are delivered from the second death. Thus Satan's power is broken. In Christ, we do not need to fear death any longer. As Jesus told Martha (John 11:25-26), "I am the resurrection and the life; he who believes in Me will live even if he dies, and everyone who lives and believes in Me will never die."

Thus, the main doctrine of our text is that Jesus became man in order to save us. He took our humanity in order to bear the penalty for our sins. But this is only true for those who are His children through the new birth, to those who believe in His name (John 1:12-13).

The use (or, application): The fact that Jesus became man to save us should cause us to draw near to Him in times of trial and to proclaim His name, even in the face of persecution.

Remember, the Book of Hebrews was written to a suffering church that was facing persecution. They were tempted to give up their profession of Christ and retreat to their old, more comfortable ways. But the author is showing them the excellency and supremacy of Jesus Christ to make the point, "You can't go back!" If Jesus is eternal God who took on human flesh to die for our salvation, you can't turn back to any other system of belief. He is God's final word to us (1:2). He entered glory only after suffering; you must be prepared to follow the same path.

The doctrines of Jesus' deity and humanity are not just nice theological points for intellectual debate. They are precious truths to sustain our souls in the trials of life! Whenever we face trials or are fearful of death, we have a personal refuge in our Brother who is our Savior! Jesus suffered in the flesh and was triumphant through His trust in God. As Hebrews 2:18 explains, "Since He Himself was tempted in that which He has suffered, He is able to come to the aid of those who are tempted."

Also, since in spite of our many sins and shortcomings, Jesus is not ashamed to call us brethren, we should not be ashamed to proclaim Him as Savior and Lord in this evil world, even if it results in persecution for us. Even if we die for our faith, we have a sure hope of being with Him throughout eternity.

Coming back to our starting point, I hope you see that sound doctrine matters greatly! As Baptists, I fear that we have gotten away from the great creeds, confessions, and catechisms that were learned verbatim by earlier generations of Christians. I close with the first question and answer of the 1563 Heidelberg Catechism (in *The Creeds of Christendom*, ed. by Philip Schaff [Baker], 3:307-308):

Question 1: What is thy only comfort in life and death?

Answer: That I, with body and soul, both in life and in death, am not my own, but belong to my faithful Savior Jesus Christ, who with his precious blood has fully satisfied for all my sins, and redeemed me from all the power of the devil; and so preserves me that without the will of my Father in heaven not a hair can fall from my head; yea, that all things must work together for my salvation. Wherefore, by his Holy Spirit, he also assures me of eternal life, and makes me heartily willing and ready henceforth to live unto him.

Application Questions

1. Some say that doctrine just leads to spiritual pride and division; thus it should not be emphasized. How would you reply?
2. Modern evangelicals are prone to believe in God as they want Him to be, not in God as revealed in His Word. What dangers does this expose us to? How can we avoid this propensity?
3. How can a believer who fears death overcome this fear?
4. Where is the proper balance between Jesus as our Brother and Jesus as the Lord to be feared?

Hebrews 2:16-18, New American Standard Bible 1995

16 For assuredly He does not give help to angels, but He gives help to the descendant of Abraham. 17 Therefore, He had to be made like His brethren in all things, so that He might become a merciful and faithful high priest in things pertaining to God, to make propitiation for the sins of the people. 18 For since He Himself was tempted in that which He has suffered, He is able to come to the aid of those who are tempted.

Why Jesus Became a Man
Hebrews 2:16-18

If we were to go out on the streets and ask people at random, "What is your greatest need?" we would probably hear a number of responses. Some would say, "My greatest need right now is to get a decent job. I can't pay my bills and get out of debt in my current situation." Others may say, "My greatest need is that I'm lonely. I need a mate or some good friends." Others might say, "My family is a war zone. My husband is abusive towards the kids and me; the kids are defiant and disrespectful. We need peace in our home."

If we went to a poor country, like India or Bangladesh, the answers to our question would center more on raw survival: "I am starving. I need food!" "I'm dying of a disease that is treatable, but I can't get the proper medicine." "I live on the streets. I need a roof over my head."

Without denying the legitimacy of any of those needs, according to the Bible, the people giving those answers are blind to their greatest need. Their greatest need is for God to forgive their sins and give them eternal life. They need to learn how to live in accordance with God's Word, so that their lives bring glory to Him. Without this focus, we could meet all of the perceived needs, but their greatest need would go unmet. If they were to die, they would spend eternity in hell.

K. P. Yohannan (told in *Revolution in World Missions* [gfa books]) grew up in India and didn't wear shoes before he was 17 (p. 55). He has preached the gospel all across India. He is not oblivious to India's oppressive poverty. But he strongly contends against getting distracted with meeting physical needs, but ignoring the spiritual needs. He says that India has seen 150 years of schools and hospitals brought to them by British missionaries, but it has not had any noticeable effect on either their churches or society (p. 103, 110).

Yohannan says that it is one of Satan's lies that people will not listen to the gospel unless we offer them something else first (p. 109). He has sat on the streets of Bombay with beggars who are about to die. He has told them that he does not have material goods to give them, but he has come to offer them eternal life, and he has seen many respond. He says (p. 111),

There is nothing wrong with charitable acts—but they are not to be confused with preaching the Gospel. Feeding programs can save a man dying from hunger. Medical aid can prolong life and fight disease. Housing projects can make this temporary life more comfortable—but only the Gospel of Jesus Christ can save a soul from a life of sin and an eternity in hell!

Thus our emphasis should always be first and foremost on evangelism and discipleship. Social concern is a result of the gospel. We must not put the cart before the horse (pp. 106, 99).

This relates directly to our text. Many would read these verses and think, "This isn't relevant to my needs. I've got to find a job. I've got to solve my personal problems. I've got a number of issues pressing in on me right now. These verses don't relate to me."

But the greatest need for us all is for a high priest to reconcile us as sinners to the holy God. Verse 17 shows how Jesus is that merciful and faithful high priest. If Jesus is your high priest, then your greatest need is to learn to live in victory over the power of sin, which will destroy your life if left unchecked. Verse 18 shows how Jesus is able to come to your aid when you are tempted.

To review, in chapter 1 the author demonstrated to his readers, who were tempted to leave Christ and go back to Judaism, how Jesus is God's final word to us. As the Son of God, He is the radiance of God's glory and the exact representation of His nature. He upholds all things by the word of His power (1:3). He is seated at the right hand of the Majesty on high, supreme over all angelic beings (1:4-14). After a brief exhortation not to drift (2:1-4), he shows that Jesus is not only the eternal Son of God, He is also fully human. God's original intent was for man to rule over the earth, but that was hindered by the fall (2:5-8). By His incarnation and death for our sins, Jesus recovered what we lost in the fall (2:9-10). As the Captain of our salvation, Jesus became man in order to bring us to God (2:11-15). Our text continues the theme of Jesus' humanity, showing us why He became a man:

Jesus became a man so that as our high priest, He could offer Himself for our sins and come to our aid when we are tempted.

He makes three points:

1. **Jesus became a man, not an angel, because He came to save people (2:16).**

The author is wrapping up his argument that he began in 2:5, that God put man on the earth to rule, and that the role of angels is "to render service for the sake of those who will inherit salvation" (1:14). The word "for" (2:16) relates to the previous two verses, about Jesus freeing us from the power and fear of death. There is debate about the meaning of the word translated, "give help." It literally means, "to take hold of" (NASB, margin). It is used of Jesus taking hold of Peter when he was sinking after walking on the water (Matt.14:31; see also Mark 8:23). It is also used in a spiritual sense of taking hold of or appropriating eternal life (1 Tim. 6:12, 19). So the debate is, in 2:16 does it refer to Jesus' taking hold of His people in the sense of helping them? Or, does it refer to His taking hold of human nature, in the sense of 2:14a?

The early church fathers uniformly interpreted it to refer to Jesus' taking hold of human nature in the incarnation (Philip Hughes, *A Commentary on the Epistle to the Hebrews* [Eerdmans], p. 115). In this sense, the verse means, "Jesus did not take to Himself the nature of angels, but rather He took on the seed of Abraham," that is, He became a Jew in fulfillment of God's covenant promise to Abraham. About the 17th century, some commentators began to interpret the verse to mean that Jesus does not give help or assistance to angels, but rather to people. In this view, "the seed of Abraham" refers to those who are Abraham's true children by faith in Jesus Christ (Gal. 3:7).

The difference does not seem that great to me. The first view emphasizes the *fact* of the incarnation, whereas the second emphasizes its *purpose*. The extended context discusses both the fact and the purpose of the incarnation. Thus I understand the sense of the verse in context to be: While the Messiah is God, and thus superior to the angels, He also had to become man so that He could suffer and die for our salvation. He did this in fulfillment of God's promise to Abraham, that through his seed, He would bless all peoples. So don't look to any angelic Messiah, and don't despise the fact that Jesus suffered and died. He had to do this to atone for our sins.

Before we move on, let me point out that this verse refutes an objection raised by those who deny the doctrine of God's sovereign election. They argue that if God does not choose everyone, then He is unloving and unjust (C. H.

Spurgeon refutes this error in his sermon, "Men Chosen—Fallen Angels Rejected," *New Park Street Pulpit* [Baker], 2:293; Dave Hunt promotes this error in *What Love is This?* [Loyal], pp. 111-112, 114-115). If they are wrong, they are also guilty of blasphemy, because they are accusing the Sovereign God of being unloving and unjust!

They *are* wrong, for at least two reasons. First, it is plain from Scripture and history that God did not make His salvation equally available to all people in all places. He chose Abraham, but not Abraham's extended family and not anyone else in any other place on earth. He later chose Abraham's descendants through Isaac and Jacob, not because they were more deserving than others, but simply because He chose to do it (Deut. 7:6-8). This meant that God chose to reject Ishmael, Esau, and their descendants (Deut. 7:1-5). As far as Scripture reveals, all the other peoples in the world in the centuries before Christ only had the general witness of creation, which is not sufficient for salvation. God permitted them to go their own ways, but He didn't reveal to them the truth about the Savior to come, as He did for the Jews (Acts 14:16-17).

Second, our text makes it clear that God did not provide for nor offer salvation to fallen angels (2 Pet. 2:4; Jude 6). He could have devised a way to offer salvation to the angels that joined Satan in his rebellion, but in His sovereign purpose, He chose not to do this. Would we dare say that this negates His love and justice? Can the fallen angels bring a charge against God because He didn't give them a way out of their condemnation? Of course not! And neither should rebellious people claim that God is unloving or unjust if He chooses some as vessels of mercy, but demonstrates His wrath and power on others as vessels of wrath prepared for destruction. As the Potter, He is free to do with the clay whatever He chooses to do, and we are not free to challenge Him (Rom. 9:19-24). I contend that the main problem with those who reject God's sovereign election is not just deficient theology. They are not in submission to God's claim to be the sovereign over His creation.

So, the author's main point in 2:16 is that Jesus became a man, not an angel. As the next verse makes clear, He did it to provide salvation to people.

2. Jesus became fully human for a specific purpose, to become a high priest to offer Himself for our sins (2:17).

Verse 17 makes three points:

A. Jesus became fully human for a specific purpose.

The verse reads, literally, "Therefore, He was obligated to be made like His brethren in all things, ..." The obligation relates to the purpose that the rest of the verse delineates, so that He might become a merciful and faithful high priest, to make propitiation for the sins of the people. And, as verse 18 states, as a result of His complete humanity, which included His being tempted, He is able to come to the aid of those who are tempted.

But the significant words in this opening phrase are, "in all things." This refutes the Docetic heresy, that Jesus only *seemed* or *appeared* to be human. No, He adopted a complete human nature, yet without sin (4:15). His body had normal human needs (for food, rest, etc.), human emotions (although not sinful emotions), and human limitations (His body was not omnipresent, although in His deity He is omnipresent). A. W. Pink (*Commentary on Hebrews* [Ephesians Four Group], vol. 1) states firmly that since Jesus was not subject to sin, He was not subject to illness. I'm not sure that this is a necessary inference, since He did live in this fallen world (harmful germs are a result of the fall) and He was subject to death. So I don't know if Jesus ever had a cold or the flu. But clearly God protected Him from any illness that would have hindered His accomplishing His ministry.

B. Jesus is our merciful and faithful high priest in the things pertaining to God.

This is the first mention of Jesus as our high priest in Hebrews, which is the only book in the New Testament to mention this truth. It is a vital concept for us to grasp, but we are at a disadvantage in that we did not grow up under the Jewish system. The Jews knew that they could not approach God directly. They had to come to Him through the priest, who would offer their sacrifices on their behalf. He represented them in everything pertaining to God. Once a year, on the Day of Atonement, the high priest would represent the entire nation by entering the Holy of Holies and presenting the blood on the mercy seat. If anyone else dared to enter that sacred place, or even if the high priest went in there on any other occasion, it meant instant death (Lev. 16:2). Thus the role of the high priest was essential so that the nation could be cleansed from its sins each year (Lev. 16:30).

Have you ever thought about what an expensive hassle it would have been to be required to bring a sacrifice to the priest every time you sinned? It would have been embarrassing, too! All the neighbors stop to look up from what they're doing as you trudge toward the tabernacle with your sacrifice. "There goes Steve again! You'd think he would learn! I wonder what he did this time?" But, as our author will develop later, Jesus offered His own blood once and for all, so that there is no need for continuing sacrifices (7:27; 9:12; 10:11-14). This must have been a *huge* relief to believing Jews! Jesus is our permanent, final high priest, who offered Himself once and for all for our sins! Thank God!

But He wasn't just any kind of high priest. He is a *merciful* high priest. That describes His motive in going to the cross (Hughes, p. 120). He had compassion on us as sinners. This means that we should never hesitate to draw near to our Lord for fear of rejection, or for fear that He will not understand. Although He will discipline us as a loving Father for our good (12:5-11), He is never harsh or lacking in compassion. As David put it (Ps. 103:13, 14), "Just as a father has compassion on his children, so the Lord has compassion on those who fear Him. For He Himself knows our frame; He is mindful that we are but dust."

John Calvin (*Calvin's Commentaries* [Baker], on Hebrews, p. 75) explains that a priest needed to be merciful so that he could help the miserable, raise up the fallen, and relieve the oppressed. Jesus, of course, did not need any experience to become merciful, but the trials that He endured assure us that He understands our trials. As Calvin puts it, "it is a rare thing for those who are always happy to sympathize with the sorrows of others." He adds (*ibid.*), "Therefore whenever any evils pass over us, let it ever occur to us, that nothing happens to us but what the Son of God has himself experienced in order that he might sympathize with us; nor let us doubt but that he is at present with us as though he suffered with us."

Jesus was also a *faithful* high priest. This refers to His faithful obedience to God in all things, culminating in His perfect obedience in going to the cross. He always trusted in and obeyed the Father, even to the point of death on the cross. You can trust in a faithful person completely. He will never let you down. So the character of Jesus as merciful and faithful invites us to draw near to Him in our every need. But that is especially true in the greatest need that every person faces:

> C. Jesus' offering of Himself on the cross satisfied God's wrath for our sins.

He became fully human "to make propitiation for the sins of the people." The NIV translates it "atonement"; the RSV has "expiation." Atonement and expiation refer to the cancellation of sin, whereas propitiation refers to the turning away of God's wrath. John Owen pointed out that there are four elements in propitiation (*An Exposition of Hebrews* [The National Foundation for Christian Education], on Heb. 2:17, p. 476): (1) an offence or crime to be taken away; (2) a person offended, to be pacified or reconciled; (3) a person offending, to be pardoned; and, (4) a sacrifice or other means of making atonement.

The notion of God's wrath is not popular. User-friendly churches don't mention it. Liberals argue that it was borrowed from the pagan idea of appeasing an angry god with a sacrifice. But it occurs no less than 585 times in the Old Testament, and more than 30 times in the New Testament (Leon Morris, "Propitiation," in *Evangelical Dictionary of Theology*, ed. by Walter Elwell [Baker], p. 888). Jesus often spoke in frightful terms about the future judgment (Mark 9:48; Luke 16:19-31). The Gospel of John (3:36) speaks of the wrath of God abiding on the one who does not obey the Son. Paul spoke often of God's wrath (Rom. 1:18, plus nine other times in Romans; 2 Thess. 1:7-9). The Book of Revelation is filled with horrifying images of the wrath of the Lamb (6:16).

God's wrath is not an angry outburst, but rather His active, settled hatred and opposition to everything evil, arising out of His holy nature. The Bible states that God not only hates sin; He also hates sinners (Ps. 5:5; 11:5). While as fallen sinners, we are to love even our enemies (Luke 6:27), we also are warned with some to "have mercy with fear, hating even the garment polluted by the flesh" (Jude 23). We who love the Lord are commanded to hate evil (Ps. 97:10).

The important point is that if we diminish the wrath of God against all sin, we also diminish the love of God for His people. What God's holy justice required, His love and mercy provided, in that "while we were yet sinners, Christ died for us" (Rom. 5:8). As Philip Hughes exclaims (p. 120),

Our hell he made his, that his heaven might be ours. Never was there such mercy, never such faithfulness, as this!

So we must hold firmly to the biblical idea that Jesus became a man to offer Himself as the perfect sacrifice that the wrath of God demands for our sins.

The chapter ends with a practical consequence of Jesus' becoming a man:

3. **Because Jesus became a man, He is able to come to our aid when we are tempted (2:18).**

Because Jesus was fully human, He was fully tempted, although not in the same sense as we who have a sin nature. He was tempted in the same sense that Adam and Eve were tempted before the fall. We would be wrong to assume that because Jesus never fell into sin, He doesn't understand the depths of our temptations. As Hughes explains (p. 124),

> [Jesus] knows the full force of temptation in a manner that we who have not withstood it to the end cannot know it. What good would another who has failed be to us? It is precisely because we have been defeated that we need the assistance of him who is the victor.

The Greek verb translated "come to the aid" means to run to the aid of those who cry out for help. Imagine a parent who hears his or her child cry out, "Help me!" We would drop what we were doing and run to help our child. That is the picture here of our merciful high priest. It also means that we are responsible to cry out to Him when we are tempted, and to flee temptation when necessary. God's Word promises (1 Cor. 10:13), "No temptation has overtaken you but such as is common to man; and God is faithful, who will not allow you to be tempted beyond what you are able, but with the temptation will provide the way of escape also, so that you will be able to endure it."

Conclusion

What is your greatest need? I hope that you see that your greatest need is to be reconciled to the holy God. Have you come to Jesus in faith that He is your propitiation, the one who bore the penalty that you deserve? If not, the wrath of God abides on you! Do not rest until your faith is in Jesus as your high priest!

If you do know Him as your high priest, are you crying out to Him for help when you are tempted? Do you know experientially the consistent deliverance from sin that is yours in Christ? He is your merciful and faithful high priest in things pertaining to God. He is able to come to your aid when you are tempted!

Application Questions

1. What is the biblical answer to the charge that God is not fair if He does not choose everyone for salvation?

2. Why is it essential to affirm Jesus' full humanity? What are the practical ramifications?

3. Why is it essential to hold to the doctrine of God's wrath against all sin? What do we lose if we compromise here?

4. Where is the balance between God's responsibility and ours when it comes to overcoming temptation?

Hebrews 3:1-6, New American Standard Bible 1995

3:1: Therefore, holy brethren, partakers of a heavenly calling, consider Jesus, the Apostle and High Priest of our confession; 2 He was faithful to Him who appointed Him, as Moses also was in all His house. 3 For He has been counted worthy of more glory than Moses, by just so much as the builder of the house has more honor than the house. 4 For every house is built by someone, but the builder of all things is God. 5 Now Moses was faithful in all His house as a servant, for a testimony of those things which were to be spoken later; 6 but Christ was faithful as a Son over His house—whose house we are, if we hold fast our confidence and the boast of our hope firm until the end.

To Endure, Consider Jesus
Hebrews 3:1-6

Most of us have made New Year's resolutions that we didn't keep. It's easy to begin a diet, but it's tough to stick to it when tempting foods are set before you! It's easy to begin an exercise program, but it's not so easy to work out when your body is screaming, "You deserve a break today!"

Or, more seriously, it's easy to begin a marriage. You're in love, you're young, you're healthy, and you think, "How could I ever have problems with this wonderful person?" But as we who have been married for many years know, it's not so easy to sustain a loving marriage when the problems of life press in.

The same is true of the Christian life. It's easy to trust in Christ and receive eternal life as a free gift. Such a deal! In our culture, it's usually easy to confess your faith in Christ through baptism. In Muslim or Hindu cultures, it can mean giving up your family and friends, and perhaps your life. But in America at present, it's fairly easy to be baptized. At first it's easy to join a local church. It's wonderful to be a part of a loving body of believers.

But, as those of us who have been Christians for a while know, it's not easy to endure. The Christian life is warfare against the powers of darkness, and there are many casualties. Yielding to sin brings down many. Others drift gradually, neglecting to spend time daily with the Lord. The crud of the world gradually builds up, like the salt and dirt on our cars during the winter months when it's difficult to wash them. Soon they are far from the Lord.

Others seem to do well for a while, but they lose their first love and settle into a humdrum Christian existence. Others fall away because they get wounded by fellow Christians who spread half-truths about them, or who treat them poorly. At first they claim to be following Jesus, but their bitterness towards His body, the church, takes a toll. They do not endure.

The Hebrew Christians had begun well. Early in their Christian experience they endured great suffering and persecution. Many had their property confiscated on account of their faith, and they endured it joyfully (10:32-34). But now they were in danger of drifting back into Judaism and neglecting their great salvation in Jesus Christ (2:1-4). So the author is exhorting them to endure. In our text, his message is simple:

To endure, consider Jesus.

"Consider" means to think about something by taking the time to observe it carefully. Jesus used the word when He told us to consider the ravens and the lilies (Luke 12:24, 27). We see ravens almost every day, but we don't usually stop to *consider* them. Jesus pointed out that they do not sow nor reap. They have no storerooms or barns, and yet God feeds them. He concludes, "How much more valuable you are than the birds!" Why didn't I think of that? Because I didn't stop to *consider* the ravens!

To consider something requires *time* and *effort*. It doesn't happen automatically, especially when you're busy. But if you take the time to do it, it usually yields rich rewards. We had some friends in California who visited Yosemite. They had heard us raving about its beauty. They told us later that they spent an hour there, saw it, and left. We were stunned! An hour in Yosemite?

I later read about an old park ranger there who was still working in his late eighties. He had literally spent his life exploring and enjoying the spectacular beauty of Yosemite. One day a citified woman hurriedly approached him and asked, "If you had only one hour to see Yosemite, what would you do?" He slowly repeated her words, "Only one hour to see Yosemite." After a pause, he said, "Ma'am, if I only had one hour to see Yosemite, I'd go over to that log, sit down, and cry!"

How much time did you spend this past week considering the beauty of Jesus Christ? The Bible has page after page revealing His majestic glory. It is our only source of information, by the way. Some Christians make up a "Jesus" in their minds, but He isn't the Jesus of the Bible. Their Jesus is nice and never judgmental. When they sin, which is often, their Jesus just hugs them and assures them that we all make mistakes. Their Jesus loves them just as they are, which is how they like it, because they don't want to confront their sins and discipline themselves for the purpose of godliness. The problem is, their "Jesus" isn't the Jesus of the Bible!

And so our antidote to drifting and our strength for endurance is to see and savor Jesus Christ from His Word. I implore myself first, because I'm prone to drift, and I implore you: *Take time to consider Jesus often!*

1. Consider Jesus as the Apostle and High Priest of our confession.

"Our confession" refers both to the body of Christian truth that we call "the faith," and to our heartfelt consent to this truth. The great creeds and confessions of Christian doctrine define in a concise way what we believe. We verbally and from the heart confess that we believe these things. The author mentions two truths about Jesus to consider:

A. Consider Jesus as the Apostle of our confession.

This is the only time in Scripture that this title is applied to Jesus. The name "Jesus" used alone focuses on the humanity of our Savior, which the author has just developed in chapter 2. As a man, born of the virgin Mary, Jesus came to earth in obedience to the Father to fulfill a specific purpose.

"Apostle" literally means, one who is sent under authority. The Gospel of John often refers to Jesus as being sent by the Father (John 3:17, 34; 5:36-38; and others). He came to reveal the Father to us and to accomplish the Father's purpose, to redeem us by shedding His blood. Jesus said that He did nothing on His own initiative, but He only sought the will of the one who sent Him (John 5:30).

We cannot know God except through Jesus (Luke 10:22). We cannot know about heaven and eternal life, except that One who eternally dwelled there left His glory there and came to reveal these things. Jesus prayed (John 17:6), "I have manifested Your name to the men whom You gave Me out of the world." We have the inspired record of what these men saw and heard in the New Testament. Jesus told the disciples after His resurrection (Luke 24:44), "all things which are written about Me in the Law of Moses and the Prophets and the Psalms must be fulfilled." Those are the three divisions of the Hebrew Bible. Thus the Old and New Testaments point to Jesus, the one who was sent under God's authority to reveal Him and to accomplish His will.

B. Consider Jesus as the High Priest of our confession.

The author already mentioned this in 2:17 and will develop it at length later. Here he only mentions it in passing, and so will I. The Apostle of our faith brings God down to us; the High Priest brings us up to God. He presented His blood on the mercy seat as the propitiation for our sins, thus satisfying the just wrath of God, so that we are now welcome in His presence.

Although he was never called an apostle, in function Moses fulfilled that role in Israel. God sent Moses under authority to deliver His people from bondage in Egypt. But Moses was not a high priest. That role fell to his brother, Aaron. Jesus fulfills both roles in one. He is our Apostle and High Priest. We must submit to His commands as the authority of God Almighty. We must come before God only through the merits of Jesus' blood. Think often and carefully of Jesus, the Apostle and High Priest of our confession!

2. Consider Jesus as greater than Moses.

From verse 2 through 6b, the author develops the theme that Jesus is greater than Moses. To understand this, you must realize that for the Jews, there was no greater leader than Moses. For them, he was the greatest man in history. God had miraculously preserved Moses' life as a little baby. God revealed Himself to Moses at the burning bush and sent him to deliver His people from centuries of bondage in Egypt. God used Moses to bring the plagues on Egypt and to part the Red Sea for the deliverance of the Jews. He struck the rock in the wilderness to provide water. He went up on the mountain to commune face to face with God and receive the Ten Commandments. God gave Moses the elaborate instructions for the Tabernacle. Moses wrote the first five books of the Old Testament, showing Israel how to live before God.

On one occasion, even Moses' brother and sister, Aaron and Miriam, challenged his leadership. God came down in a pillar of cloud and said (Num. 12:6-8),

> Hear now My words: If there is a prophet among you, I, the Lord, shall make myself known to him in a vision. I shall speak with him in a dream. Not so, with My servant Moses. He is faithful in all My household; with him I speak mouth to mouth, even openly, and not in dark sayings, and he beholds the form of the Lord. Why then were you not afraid to speak against My servant, against Moses?

When the cloud had lifted, Miriam had become leprous! Moses graciously cried out to God to heal her, which He did. In all of the history of the Jews, there was none greater or held in higher esteem than Moses.

But Moses was not perfect, and the author could have focused on his mistakes. But he does not do that. Instead, he begins by showing that…

A. Both Jesus and Moses were faithful men (3:2).

Twice (3:2, 5) the author cites Numbers 12:7, that Moses was faithful in all God's house. As Paul said (1 Cor. 4:2), "it is required of stewards that one be found [faithful]" (same Greek word). A faithful man lives all of life, including his inner thought life, with a God-ward focus. As Paul told the Thessalonians (1 Thess. 2:3-6), he didn't come to them with flattering speech or a pretext for greed. Then he interjected, "God is witness." Paul said that he spoke, "not as pleasing men, but God who examines our hearts." He knew that God knows our every thought and motive. So he wasn't playing to the crowds. He sought to please God in everything that he did, whether in public or in private. That is the key to being faithful.

The author's point here is that both Jesus and Moses were faithful men. He compares rather than contrasts them because he knew that his audience thought highly of Moses and because God Himself commends Moses as a faithful man. In Exodus 35-40, there are 22 references to Moses' faithfulness to God (John MacArthur, Jr., *Hebrews* [Moody Press], p. 82). Jesus, of course, was more faithful than anyone, including Moses, because He never failed even once. But the author begins with this comparison. Then he goes on to show how Jesus is greater than Moses.

B. Jesus is worthy of more glory than Moses, as the builder of the house is greater than the house (3:3-4).

The main point here is that although Moses was a great leader, he was just a member of God's house, but Jesus was the builder. Verse 4 clarifies that God is the builder of all things. Since Jesus is the builder of God's house (2:3), Jesus is God. As the author began this epistle, it was through Jesus that God made the world (1:3).

So without in any way demeaning Moses, who was a great leader, the author is saying, "Jesus is in a totally different class! Moses was a faithful leader in God's house, but Jesus built the house. If you marvel at how Israel became a nation after 400 years in slavery, and you're amazed at how God used Moses to lead them out of Egypt, marvel still more at the fact that it was Jesus who designed the whole program! He called Abraham out of Ur of the Chaldees and promised to bless all nations through his descendants. He revealed Himself to Moses in the burning bush. He was with Israel in the wilderness in the pillar and cloud. He fed them with manna and gave them water from the rock (see 1 Cor. 10:1-4). While Moses is worthy of honor, Jesus is worthy of far more glory. So don't turn back from Jesus to following Moses or you'll be turning from God Himself to mere man."

    C. Moses was faithful as a servant over God's house, but Jesus was faithful as the Son (3:5-6).

The Greek word for "servant" is used only here in the New Testament. It comes from the Septuagint of Numbers 12:7 and has the nuance of one who serves voluntarily (G. Abbott-Smith, *A Manual Greek Lexicon of the New Testament* [Charles Scribner's Sons], p. 108). The contrast is, although Moses was great, he was only a servant, whereas Jesus is the Son of God, the heir of all things.

As a servant, Moses' role was to testify "of those things which were to be spoken later" (3:5). All that Moses wrote looked ahead to Jesus, who rebuked the Pharisees, saying (John 5:46), "If you believed Moses, you would believe Me, for he wrote about Me." Moses was just a servant, pointing ahead to the heir, who is Jesus. And so the argument is, "Don't go back to Moses. Consider Jesus, because He is greater than Moses."

Probably none of us are tempted to turn back to Moses, but we are easily tempted to turn to good things in such a way that we miss the best. Some believers emphasize obedience, and certainly obedience is a good thing. God forbid that we do not obey His Word! But sometimes those who emphasize obedience start adding things that go beyond God's Word and they fall into legalism. They camp on minor issues, but neglect the majors. They push man-made rules or standards as if they were binding on all Christians. They take pride in their conformity to these rules and look down on those who don't keep them. Jesus confronted the Pharisees, who were meticulous about tithing even their table spices, but who neglected "the weightier provisions of the law: justice and mercy and faithfulness" (Matt. 23:23).

I have seen others who emphasize Bible knowledge or correct theology, and again, those are very important things. But if our Bible knowledge and theology do not lead us to know and worship Jesus Christ more fully and to submit our hearts more completely to Him, we've traded the best for the good. If we take pride in our great knowledge and look down on those who are not as enlightened as we are, we're off track. True knowledge of the supremacy of Jesus leads to humility, not pride.

So, consider Jesus! To endure the many trials and temptations of the Christian walk, consider Jesus as the Apostle and High Priest of our confession. Consider Jesus as greater than Moses.

3. Consider also what Jesus had made us.

It is significant how the author addresses his readers:

A. Jesus has made us "holy brethren" (3:1).

The name "brethren" probably points back to 2:11, where he said that Jesus is not ashamed to call His people brethren. It brings out the close relationship that we enjoy with our Savior. The adjective "holy" looks back to the same verse, where he says that Jesus is the one who sanctifies and we are the sanctified. Both terms come from the word that is translated "holy." It refers to those who are set apart unto God from the world. The apostle Paul often addresses God's people as "saints," which means, "holy ones." "Saints" are not a special class of extraordinary Christians, who deserve special recognition. All who know Jesus Christ as Savior and Lord are saints or "holy brethren."

There are three senses of sanctification, or holiness. In the sense we are considering, we have once for all been set apart unto God at the moment of salvation. In an ongoing sense, we are progressively being sanctified as we grow in godliness. In the future sense, when we see Jesus, we will be totally sanctified forever, so that we will never again sin. If we would keep in mind our present position as saints or holy brethren, it would help us to say no to temptation and to live as people who are set apart unto God.

B. Jesus has made us partakers of a heavenly calling (3:1).

The author of Hebrews uses the word "heavenly" more often than any other New Testament book (6 times: 3:1; 6:4 [gift]; 8:5 [sanctuary]; 9:23 [things]; 11:16 [country]; 12:22 [Jerusalem]). Donald Guthrie writes, (*Hebrews, Tyndale New Testament Commentaries* [IVP/ Eerdmans], p. 97), "In all cases, the 'heavenly' is contrasted with the earthly, and in all cases the heavenly is the superior, the real as compared with the shadow." Our calling is heavenly in that it comes from heaven and it culminates in heaven. The initiative comes from God, who calls us to be His "called-out ones" (*ekklesia*, the Greek word for "church"). To be partakers of a heavenly calling means that our focus must be on heaven and the blessings God has promised us there, not on the things of this earth (Col. 3:1-4).

C. Jesus has made us His house (3:6).

"House" is used seven times in this paragraph. It is a metaphor for God's people, in whom He dwells (Eph. 2:19, 22; 1 Tim. 3:15; 1 Pet. 2:4-5). The Bible never calls a church building "God's house." God's *people* are His house. They may gather in a barn or an open field or a house or a building constructed specifically for worship. But the building isn't sacred; the people are sacred! We are to be built *together* into a holy temple of the Lord, a dwelling of God in the Spirit (Eph. 2:21-22).

All of this is very comforting, but then the author throws in one of those uncomfortable warnings: "*if* we hold fast our confidence and the boast of our hope." (The phrase, "firm until the end" was probably not original and was inserted from 3:14; Bruce Metzger, *A Textual Commentary on the Greek New Testament* [United Bible Societies], second ed., p. 595). F. F. Bruce explains the "if" clause (*Commentary on the Epistle to the Hebrews* [Eerdmans], p. 59):

> Nowhere in the New Testament more than [Hebrews] do we find such repeated insistence on the fact that continuance in the Christian life is the test of reality. The doctrine of the final perseverance of the saints has as its corollary the salutary teaching that the saints are the people who persevere to the end."

He goes on to cite the parable of the sower, where the seed thrown on the rocky ground made a good showing at first, but then faded away in the hot sun, because it had no deep roots. Jesus interpreted this to refer to those who welcome the word with joy at first, but are only temporary, because "when affliction or persecution arises because of the word, immediately they fall away" (Mark 4:17). As Bruce explains, this is precisely what the author of Hebrews fears will happen with his readers. Thus he emphasizes repeatedly the need for bold confidence and joyful hope.

Conclusion

The Christian life is not a 100-yard dash; it's a marathon. That name comes from the decisive Battle of Marathon, where the Greeks fought the Persians. If the Persians had conquered, the glory that was Greece never would have been known. Against fearful odds, the Greeks won the battle. A Greek soldier ran all the way, day and night, to Athens with the news. He ran straight to the magistrates and gasped, "Rejoice, we have conquered!" Then he dropped dead. He had completed his mission and done his work (William Barclay, *The Letters to Timothy, Titus, and Philemon* [Westminster Press], pp. 210-211).

It is significant that when Paul wrote his final letter to Timothy, he did not report on how many he had won to Christ, how many churches he had planted, or how many evangelistic campaigns he had conducted. He said simply (2 Tim. 4:7), "I have fought the good fight, I have finished the course, I have kept the faith." He fought and he finished—he endured! If you want to join his ranks, take time often to consider Jesus.

Application Questions

1. Why is important to derive our understanding of Jesus from the Bible *alone*, not from personal experience or popular ideas?

2. What are some practical ramifications of Jesus being the Apostle of our confession?

3. What are some practical ramifications of Jesus being greater than Moses?

4. Many Christians are bitter towards the church and prefer to worship "outside" the church. Why is this not God's plan?

Hebrews 3:7-11, New American Standard Bible 1995

7 Therefore, just as the Holy Spirit says,

> "Today if you hear His voice,
> 8 Do not harden your hearts as when they provoked Me,
> As in the day of trial in the wilderness,
> 9 Where your fathers tried Me by testing Me,
> And saw My works for forty years.
> 10 "Therefore I was angry with this generation,
> And said, 'They always go astray in their heart,
> And they did not know My ways';
> 11 As I swore in My wrath,
> 'They shall not enter My rest.'"

A Warning Against Hardness of Heart
Hebrews 3:7-11

If you have been a Christian for very long, you have watched someone make a profession of faith in Christ, followed by dramatic changes in his life. It's exciting to see his new joy. But then a difficult trial hits. His faith is shaken. He stops coming to church and begins to avoid other Christians. Soon he is back into his old ways. And you wonder, "What happened? Was his conversion genuine? Can Christians lose their salvation?"

Jesus explained what I just described in the parable of the sower. He said that the seed of the gospel falls on four kinds of soils: the hard road; the thin soil over a hard rocky layer; the soil infested with thorns; and, the good soil. I just described the seed that fell on the rocky soil. In Jesus' words (Mark 4:16-17), "When they hear the word, immediately [they] receive it with joy; and they have no firm root in themselves, but are only temporary; then, when affliction or persecution arises because of the word, immediately they fall away." Neither they nor the thorny ground persevere to bear fruit unto eternal life.

The author of Hebrews is concerned that his readers may be the rocky soil that withers under affliction or persecution. They were in danger of going back to a more comfortable life in their old Jewish religion because of the imminent threat of persecution in their newfound Christian faith. So as he concludes his comparison showing Jesus' superiority over Moses, he says that we are God's house, but then adds (3:6), "if we hold fast our confidence and the boast of our hope."

He continues by illustrating his point with the story of Israel in the wilderness, a story that all of his readers knew well. He quotes the latter half of Psalm 95, which in its entirety was the call to worship in the Jewish synagogues. It tells about a people who had been redeemed from Egypt by applying the blood of the Passover lamb to their homes. They had been "baptized" into Moses through the cloud that enveloped them and through the Red Sea (1 Cor. 10:2). They had eaten the heavenly manna and drank water from the rock. Seemingly, they were a "redeemed" people. Yet, as Paul states (1 Cor. 10:5), "with most of them God was not well-pleased; for they were laid low in the wilderness." As he goes on to say, "these things happened as examples," so that we would not fall into their same sins.

The author of Hebrews uses this story to make the same point. He is warning us against the soul-destroying sin of hardness of heart. He is saying,

To avoid hardness of heart, we must submit our hearts to God's Word and God's ways, especially in times of trial.

We can divide our text into four lessons:

1. To avoid hardness of heart, we must submit to God's authority through His inspired Word.

He begins (3:7), "Therefore, just as the Holy Spirit says," and then quotes from Psalm 95. In 4:7, he mentions that David was the human author of the psalm, but here he emphasizes that it was really the Holy Spirit who spoke and who continues to speak to us ("says" is present tense). This means:

A. What the Bible says, God is saying to us now.

Although the author isn't directly speaking to the issue of the inspiration of Scripture, his attributing Psalm 95 to the Holy Spirit shows his implicit belief that God inspired Scripture. The Holy Spirit used human authors, but He is the divine voice behind all Scripture. As Peter explains (2 Pet. 1:21), "no prophecy was ever made by an act of human will, but men moved by the Holy Spirit spoke from God." Or, as Paul puts it (literally, 2 Tim. 3:16), "All Scripture is God-breathed." Charles Hodge (*Systematic Theology* [Eerdmans], 1:154) wrote,

> On this subject the common doctrine of the Church is, and ever has been, that inspiration was an influence of the Holy Spirit on the minds of certain select men, which rendered them the organs of God for the infallible communication of his mind and will. They were in such a sense the organs of God, that what they said God said.

The starting point for avoiding a hardened heart is to recognize and submit to God's authority through His inspired Word. If we sit in judgment on the Word, criticizing the things we don't agree with as outdated or in error, our hearts are challenging God. To learn from God, we must submit to His inspired Word.

B. We should learn from the biblical stories how to avoid the sins of those who lived before us.

As Paul says (1 Cor. 10:11), these things "were written for our instruction." We disobey or ignore them to our own peril. The starting point is that we *hear His voice* (Heb. 3:7). "To hear" in Hebrew often has the nuance of not just hearing sounds, but also of obeying what we hear. In this regard, it is amazing how many Christians never read the Old Testament. They are unfamiliar with the many stories of triumph and tragedy that are recorded there for our instruction in the faith.

The story behind Psalm 95 (Heb. 3:7-11) is recorded in Exodus 17. Israel had just come out of Egypt through God's mighty deliverance. They went three days into the wilderness and found no water, except bitter water. Did the people say, "Well, God didn't go to all the trouble of delivering us from Egypt so that we would thirst to death in this desert"? No, they grumbled at Moses. He cried out to God, who showed him a tree. When he threw it into the water, it became sweet (Exod. 15:22-25). Exodus 16 tells how God provided manna to feed Israel each day.

You would think that after these gracious miracles, the people would have implicitly trusted God. But then you come to Exodus 17, when again they came to a place where there was no water. Rather than asking God to provide, the people quarreled with Moses and put God to the test. God instructed Moses to strike a rock with his staff, and water gushed forth. Moses named that place Massah (= a test) and Meribah (= a quarrel). The Greek translates the Hebrew, "as at Meribah," into, "as when they provoked Me" (3:8a). It translates, "As in the day of Massah," into, "as in the day of trial" (3:8b).

The last part of the Psalm, referring to God's swearing in wrath that they would not enter His rest, probably refers to Numbers 14, when the people grumbled after the report of the spies. In spite of all that God had done, they were ready to stone Moses and return to Egypt, when God intervened. On that occasion, He swore that all that had grumbled against Him would die in the wilderness, and thus not enter the land of rest. Only Joshua and Caleb, who believed God, were spared. The point is, we should learn from their sins and do differently!

C. God's Word speaks directly to us today.

Says is in the present tense. "*Today*, if you hear His voice…" This very day, God speaks to us through His Word! *Today* lends a sense of urgency to this message. It says, "Don't put off obedience to a more convenient time. *Now* is the day of salvation! Now is the time God is speaking to you. Don't ignore Him! You may not get another opportunity!"

We have to apply Scripture to our lives in line with proper rules of interpretation, or we may misapply it. Before we apply it to ourselves, we need to figure out what it was saying to the original hearers in their historical context. We need to compare Scripture with Scripture, and interpret the text in its context. For example, we are not under the Jewish laws of sacrifice or cleansing. But there are lessons in these things that do apply to us who have seen the fulfillment of them in Christ. To sum up this point: to avoid hardness of heart, we must come to God's Word with submissive hearts, ready to obey His will.

2. **To avoid hardness of heart, we must make sure that our hearts are in proper relationship to God.**

Note 3:8, "Do not harden your *hearts*," and, 3:10, "They always go astray in their *hearts*." In the Bible, the heart refers to our total inner being—the mind, the emotions, and the will. As Proverbs 4:23 warns us, "Watch over your heart with all diligence, for from it flow the springs of life."

A. All sin begins in the heart.

Jesus taught (Mark 7:21-22), "For from within, out of the heart of men, proceed the evil thoughts, fornications, thefts, murders, adulteries, deeds of coveting and wickedness, as well as deceit, sensuality, envy, slander, pride and foolishness." We tend to look at the outward man, but God looks on the heart (1 Sam. 16:7).

For example, we see a man in ministry, who preaches God's Word. He serves the church selflessly. He seems so kind and caring. Suddenly, he falls into adultery, and we are shocked. How could this happen? We didn't see that in his heart, he was lusting after women and was not judging his sin. He was not walking in holiness before God in his thought life. What came out in his behavior stemmed from his heart. This is one of the most helpful lessons I have learned about the Christian walk: *all sin begins in the heart*. If you deal with your thought life before God, you stop sin at the root.

B. Our hardness of heart stirs up God's anger and incurs His severe judgment or discipline.

God says that He was angry with the generation in the wilderness (3:8). This word has the nuance of being disgusted with, or loathing someone. He swore in His wrath (3:11). Wrath refers to God's settled, passionate opposition to sin. God is not passive when it comes to sin. If we profess to be His children, but have not truly repented of our sins (as was the case with many who perished in the wilderness), God's eternal wrath is upon us (John 3:36). If we are truly His children through faith in Christ, then Jesus bore God's wrath for us on the cross, so that we do not need to fear His eternal punishment. But we should fear His discipline, which is never pleasant (Heb. 12:6, 11). He disciplines His children in love, that we may share His holiness. But He can get pretty rough if He has to! If we judge our own hearts, we will avoid God's discipline (1 Cor. 11:27-32).

Thus, to avoid hardness of heart, we must submit to the authority of God's Word and we must do business with God on the heart level.

3. To avoid hardness of heart, we must recognize and submit to God's ways.

God says of Israel in the wilderness (3:10), "They did not know My ways." He says (Isa. 55:8-9), "'For My thoughts are not your thoughts, nor are your ways My ways,' declares the Lord. 'For as the heavens are higher than the earth, so are My ways higher than your ways, and My thoughts than your thoughts.'" The only way that we can know God's ways are as He has revealed them to us in the Scriptures.

A. We are responsible to learn and submit to God's ways.

We can't plead ignorance. We can't protest, "But, God, I didn't know that You were working in *that* way!" These people in the wilderness should have known God's ways. But since they didn't know His ways, they didn't submit to them. The time to learn God's ways is *before* we get into a difficult situation (Prov. 1:20-33). If we neglect wisdom when we have opportunity to learn it, we will be overwhelmed when we get into a crisis without it.

B. God's ways sometimes reveal His mighty power, but miracles alone will not change a stubborn heart.

Those who went astray had seen some of the greatest miracles that God has ever done. They saw the ten plagues in Egypt. They witnessed the Red Sea part for them and close up again on Pharaoh's army. They had seen God provide water and manna already in the barren Sinai desert. God emphasizes that *for forty years* they saw His works (3:9). If miracles alone could soften hard hearts, these people should have been mighty in faith! But they weren't.

You hear people say, "If I just saw a miracle, I'd believe." Sometimes God does use miracles to bring people to saving faith. But often, those words are just a smokescreen. The skeptic is just making an excuse so that he can continue in his sin. The rich man in Hades pled with Abraham to send someone to his brothers and warn them, so that they would not come to that place of torment (Luke 16:27-31). Abraham replied, "They have Moses and the Prophets; let them hear them." The rich man replied, "No, father Abraham, but if someone goes to them from the dead, they will repent!" Just let them see a miracle! But Abraham answered, "If they do not listen to Moses and the Prophets, they will not be persuaded even if someone rises from the dead."

C. God's ways often involve situations of extreme trial for His people.

Remember, His ways are *not* our ways. He often works in an upside-down sort of way that seems strange to us. Again, His Word reveals His different ways to us so that we will recognize them when they actually happen to us.

Consider God's ways in delivering Israel from 400 years of slavery in Egypt. To pull this off, He needs a strong Jewish leader. Pick a man who has been raised in Pharaoh's household, trained in all of the wisdom of the Egyptians, a man powerful in word and deed (Acts 7:22). So far, so good! Then, have this man fail in a colossal manner and spend the next forty years of his life tending sheep out in the wilderness. Whoa! Then, when God calls him to his task, He will harden Pharaoh's heart repeatedly, so that he will make the Israelites' task harder and will refuse to let them go.

Once he lets them go, march Israel to the Red Sea, where they're helplessly trapped for Pharaoh's strong army. Once they get through this crisis, lead them out into the barren desert, where there is no water. When they find water, make it bitter water. Rather than lead them directly into the Promised Land, an eleven-day journey (Deut. 1:2), take them on the "scenic route," a forty-year journey through the barren desert. That was God's way with His chosen people! He wanted to teach them to trust Him and learn warfare (Exod. 13:17).

Regarding Canaan, God could have sent a plague to wipe out the wicked Canaanites. Israel then could have moved in and lived happily ever after. Instead, God required Israel to fight many difficult battles to get rid of the Canaanites. Later, when Israel needed a prophet, God's way was to make a woman barren. There were many women with children in Israel, but God's way was to bring a woman to desperation, where she knew that she could not produce a son. When she cried out to God, He gave her Samuel, who became His prophet (1 Samuel 1 & 2). Later, when God wanted a man after His heart to be on Israel's throne, He didn't pick the man whom Samuel would have picked. He chose the youngest of Jesse's sons, a teenage shepherd named David. Then, rather than putting him on the throne immediately, God had his chosen one run for years, in fear of his life, from the mad King Saul.

I could multiply examples, because they are all through the Bible. God's ways usually involve bringing His people to the end of themselves, so that they know that *their trust must be in Him alone* (see Psalm 107). If we do not know His ways, when we are put in the wilderness with no water, or when we are barren with no strength to produce anything for God, we will be prone to grumble, as Israel did. So we must learn to know His ways through His Word.

    D. When we are confronted with God's ways, we have the choice of submitting to Him or grumbling and going back to the world.

Psalm 95:1-3 reads,

O come, let us sing for joy to the Lord,
Let us shout joyfully to the rock of our salvation.
Let us come before His presence with thanksgiving,
Let us shout joyfully to Him with psalms.
For the Lord is a great God,
And a great King above all gods.

The warning of our text comes after seven verses of praise. The choice is clear: rejoice in the Lord by faith, or grumble and turn back to the world (Egypt).

The apostle Paul in his letter to the Philippians demonstrates the proper response to God's ways. He was in prison in Rome on false charges. Fellow Christian leaders in Rome were criticizing him and preaching out of envy. As God's great apostle to the Gentiles, Paul easily could have complained about his unfair, difficult circumstances. And yet he wrote (Phil. 2:15), "Do all things without grumbling or disputing." The words "rejoice," or "joy" occur over 15 times in this short letter. It's not a coincidence that the Greek word for "attitude" also occurs ten times. Our attitude of submission and trust in God will lead us into joy, even in the midst of great trials. An attitude of pride and self-centeredness leads to grumbling, where we resist God's ways and turn back to the world.

    E.   To refuse to submit to God's ways is to put God to the test.

God says (3:9), "your fathers tried Me by testing Me." At the root of testing God is the sin of unbelief (which we will examine in more detail in the next chapter). When God promises something and we face trials that seem to negate His promise, we again are faced with a choice: Is God faithful to His word or not? Granted, we're in a barren desert with no water. Granted, there are huge giants that live in the land. In ourselves, we are completely unable to deal with these problems. Will we trust in God and His promises, or will we allow the problems to cause us to grumble and not take God at His word? If we do not submit to God's ways and trust in His word, we put Him to the test, which is normally not a good thing to do! (There are rare exceptions; see Mal. 3:10.)

Thus, to avoid hardness of heart, we must submit to God's authority through His Word. We must make sure that our hearts are properly submitted to Him. We must recognize and submit to His ways of dealing with us. Finally,

4.   When we submit to God's Word and His ways, we enter into His rest.

We will deal with this more when we look at Hebrews 4. But for now, note 3:11. God's oath refers to His settled determination that those who rebelled in the wilderness would not enter the land of Canaan (Num. 14:21-36). When God swears in His wrath, we had better believe that He means business! There is no rest for the soul that is under God's settled wrath!

God's rest had an initial reference to Israel's settling into the land of promise, but it also has a spiritual fulfillment, as we'll see in Hebrews 4. Leon Morris

(*Expositor's Bible Commentary*, ed. by Frank Gaebelein [Zondervan], 12:35) says that God's rest refers to "a place of blessing where there is no more striving but only relaxation in the presence of God and in the certainty that there is no cause for fear." God's spiritual rest comes to the person who "does not work, but believes in Him who justifies the ungodly" (Rom. 4:5). As Romans 5:1 assures us, "Therefore, having been justified by faith, we have peace with God through our Lord Jesus Christ."

Conclusion

One of God's ways that is most unlike our ways is the cross. Jesus, the sinless Son of God died as the sacrifice for ungodly sinners. God justifies the ungodly through faith alone. That runs counter to human pride. Have you trusted in Jesus' blood alone as your hope for heaven? Is your heart in submission to God's Word and His ways, especially when those ways involve a trip through the barren wilderness? Your heart is either hardening against God because you are resisting His sovereign ways with you, or it is growing softer toward God because you are submitting to His Word and His ways. Your response to trials reveals your heart. Send down spiritual roots, deep into the fertile, moist soil of God's Word, so that you can endure when the hot sun of affliction beats down on you, as it surely will!

Application Questions

1. Since God's Word does not all apply directly to us, how can we be sure that we are applying it properly?

2. Since the sinful heart is deceitful (Jer. 17:9), how can we know when our hearts are properly submissive to God?

3. Why do God's ways often involve trials for His people? Is it wrong to pray for these trials to be lifted? Why/why not?

4. Why is grumbling about our circumstances a serious sin? What does it really reflect?

Hebrews 3:12-19, New American Standard Bible 1995

12 Take care, brethren, that there not be in any one of you an evil, unbelieving heart that falls away from the living God. 13 But encourage one another day after day, as long as it is still called "Today," so that none of you will be hardened by the deceitfulness of sin. 14 For we have become partakers of Christ, if we hold fast the beginning of our assurance firm until the end, 15 while it is said,

> "Today if you hear His voice,
> Do not harden your hearts, as when they provoked Me."

16 For who provoked Him when they had heard? Indeed, did not all those who came out of Egypt led by Moses? 17 And with whom was He angry for forty years? Was it not with those who sinned, whose bodies fell in the wilderness? 18 And to whom did He swear that they would not enter His rest, but to those who were disobedient? 19 So we see that they were not able to enter because of unbelief.

Persevering in Faith
Hebrews 3:12-19

One of the most controversial issues among Christians is, "Can a believer lose his salvation?" Our emotions can get involved, since most of us have loved ones who at one time made a profession of faith in Christ, and perhaps were even involved in some ministry. But today they are far from the Lord. We wonder, "Is this person truly saved?" Our hearts want to say "yes," but there are scary verses, such as several in our text, that make us hesitate.

Among evangelicals, there are three main camps. Consistent Arminians would say that this person was saved, but he lost his salvation. These folks view salvation primarily as a human decision. If your decision to believe gets you in, your decision to deny the faith puts you out. I dismiss this view as indefensible in light of many Scriptures that promise security to God's children (such as Rom. 8:1 & 29-36).

Among those who hold that believers cannot lose their salvation, there are two main camps. Some argue that perseverance is not necessary for salvation to be secure. Their motto is, "Once saved, always saved." They argue that if salvation requires perseverance then it depends on works. And they argue that if final salvation depends on perseverance, then assurance of salvation is impossible. What if I fall away in the future? And so they say that all that matters is that a person once believed in Christ.

This view shares with the Arminian view the idea that faith is a human decision. It is not a gift that God imparts to those He regenerates. Rather, faith is like a lever that we pull. Once we pull it, all the benefits of salvation come pouring out, and we can't stop the process. We can walk away and say that we don't want those benefits, but they still belong to us. How we live after we believe has nothing to do with our eternal destiny or security.

The other main view is that of Reformed theology, that saving faith is God's gift, imparted to us when He saves us. Salvation originates with God and depends totally on His purpose and power. Since He promises to complete what He began to the praise of His glorious grace, all of God's elect will persevere in faith unto eternal life. This view, which I believe is the truth, holds that there is such a thing as false faith. It is possible for some who profess faith in

Persevering in Faith

Christ later to fall away from the faith, thus demonstrating that their faith was not genuine. But saving faith, by its very nature, perseveres. Continuance in the faith is the evidence that our faith is from God, and not from man.

This is not to say that persevering faith is effortless or automatic. God ordains the means as well as the ends. God's sovereignty in salvation never negates human responsibility. God elects all whom He saves, but the elect are responsible to repent of their sins and believe in Jesus Christ. Although God promises that His elect will all finally be saved, we are exhorted to persevere in faith. God's sovereignty and human responsibility are not at odds!

Our text is a strong exhortation to persevere in the faith. Genuine believers will heed the warning and hold fast to their faith in times of trial. False believers will grumble against God and fall into sin and unbelief when trials hit, just as many in Israel did in the wilderness. So the author exhorts the church ("brethren," 3:12) to "hold fast the beginning of our assurance firm until the end" (3:14). He shows us four aspects of persevering faith:

To persevere in faith, there is a great sin to avoid, a great service to practice, a great salvation to hold to, and a great story to personalize.

1. To persevere in faith, there is a great sin to avoid (3:12).

If I were to ask you to name what you consider to be the very worst sins, we would probably hear mass murder, genocide, child molestation, cannibalism, and degraded sexual practices. Unbelief probably would not occur to us. But it's on God's list of terrible sins: "Take care, brethren, that there not be in any one of you an evil, unbelieving heart, …" (3:12).

A. To avoid this terrible sin, we must see how evil unbelief really is.

If we shrug it off as no big deal, we won't be on guard against it. If I told you that there is a stray cat on the loose outside, you'd say, "No big deal." You wouldn't be cautious about encountering this wild animal. But if I mentioned that the stray cat was a hungry lion, you'd be a bit more careful! Consider five aspects of unbelief that should cause us to be on guard against it:

    1) Unbelief is the worst of all sins, because it is the root of all sins.

Unbelief is behind every other sin that people commit. When Satan tempted Eve in the garden, he got her to disbelieve the word of God (Gen.

3:1): "Indeed, has God said, 'You shall not eat from any tree of the garden?'" He was saying, "You really can't believe that, can you?" If people really believed God, they would not practice any of the terrible sins mentioned earlier, because they would know that they will face His severe judgment. But not believing God, they do as they please. Unbelief is the root of all sins.

    2) Unbelief is a sin that hardens the heart.

In 3:13 the author warns that they may be hardened by this sin. He repeats the warning again in 3:15, where he cites again the verse from Psalm 95 (see 3:8). Sin is like the calluses that form on our skin. If we don't have calluses, our hands are sensitive to any pain. But once calluses form, we can do things that previously would have caused pain, and we barely feel it. Our consciences are that way. The first time we commit a sin, our conscience goes "Ouch!" The second time, it hurts, but not as bad. After a while, we can do it without even being aware that we are sinning. I've read of hardened hit men with the Mafia that can shoot a man in the face at close range and then go out for lunch to celebrate. Unbelief hardens our hearts against God's standards of holiness.

    3) Unbelief is a persistent threat to all of God's people.

In 3:13, the author tells us to "encourage one another day after day, as long as it is still called 'Today.'" He is referring back to the word "today" in Psalm 95. It warns us that this sin of unbelief is a persistent, daily threat. We may have been strong in faith yesterday, but then we run out of water in the wilderness today. How will we respond? Will we trust God and look to Him in faith to provide, or will we grumble and turn back to the world?

True believers can fall into the sin of unbelief. God had promised David that he would sit on the throne of Israel, but David was running for his life from the mad King Saul. After years of this, David said to himself (1 Sam. 27:1), "Now I will perish one day by the hand of Saul. There is nothing better for me than to escape into the land of the Philistines." That was *not* a statement of faith in God's promise! It got David into all sorts of trouble before he finally came to his senses (1 Sam. 30:6). But the point is, believers are not immune from unbelief! Be on guard!

    4) Unbelief, like all sin, deceives us.

The author refers to "the deceitfulness of sin" (3:13). Sin fools us into thinking that it will get us out of our current problems and will deliver what we want, and that obedience to God will deprive us of what we want. When David went over to the Philistines, Saul stopped pursuing him. The Philistine king gave David his own city. Instead of living from cave to cave, David and his wives could settle down in a normal way of life. Sin always works that way. It fools us into thinking that we're getting what we want. But then the bills of sin come due!

You're single and lonely. There haven't been any godly men calling you for a date. Satan comes along and says, "You'll never get what you want if you wait on God! Here's a nice unbeliever. Go out with him!" Or, you're having problems in your marriage. Your wife constantly nags you. She doesn't meet your needs sexually. Along comes a beautiful, sensitive, understanding woman who offers herself to you. Satan whispers, "She will meet your needs!" Sin, including unbelief, always deceives us.

    5) Unbelief is inseparable from disobedience.

In verse 12, the warning is against *unbelief*, but in verse 13, without any shift in subject, he warns against the deceitfulness of *sin*. In verses 17 & 18, he mentions those who *sinned* and were *disobedient*. In verse 19 he explains that they were barred from entering the land because of *unbelief*. The Bible repeatedly uses "faith" and "obedience" interchangeably (John 3:36; Acts 6:7; Rom. 1:5; 10:16; 15:18; 16:26; 2 Thess. 1:8; 1 Pet. 1:2; 2:8; 3:1; 4:17). We are saved by faith alone, but saving faith always results in a life of obedience to God (James 2:18-26). If you truly believe God, you will obey Him. If you disbelieve God, you will disobey Him.

Thus to avoid this terrible sin of unbelief, we must see how evil it really is.

    B. To avoid this terrible sin we must exercise great caution.

"Take care, brethren" (3:12)! "Look out! Be on guard!" It does not require carefulness to go to hell, but it does require great carefulness to go to heaven. If you're nonchalant or unconcerned about your soul, the powerful stream of the world, the flesh, and the devil will sweep you into hell. You must *strive* to enter at the narrow gate of heaven (Luke 13:24). Vigilance and watchfulness are marks of true believers. True believers do not flippantly say, "Hey, don't worry about a little sin! Once saved, always saved!" True believers examine their hearts often to make sure that they are in the faith (2 Cor. 13:5). They take care that their hearts do not become evil and unbelieving, so that they do not fall away from the living God.

    C. To avoid this terrible sin, we must avoid ritualistic religion and walk closely with the living God.

As we saw in the last chapter, Christianity is a matter of the heart before God. It's easy to put on a good show in front of others, so that they think, "What a godly man Steve is!" I can sing with a loud voice, I can lift my hands in worship, I can pray with intensity, I can partake of communion, and I can even preach sermons with fervency—but it could all be outward! God is the *living God* (9:14; 10:31; 12:22) who looks on the heart. Hebrews 4:13 states, "And there is no creature hidden from His sight, but all things are open and laid bare to the eyes of Him with whom we have to do." The living God knows my every doubt and sinful thought. I can't fool Him, even for a second! If I want to avoid falling into this terrible sin of unbelief, I must bring every thought captive to the obedience of Christ. I must confess my doubts as sin and walk in reality before the living God every day. To persevere in faith, there is a great sin to avoid, namely, unbelief.

2. To persevere in faith, there is a great service to practice (3:13).

"But encourage one another day after day, ..." The verb can also mean to exhort. The root word has the idea of coming alongside someone to give aid. It is used as a name for the Holy Spirit (John 14:16, 26, "Helper"). Briefly, note three things about this service or ministry of encouragement:

    A. Encouragement is a service for every member of the body.

This is not just something that pastors should do. It is a necessary ministry for every member of the body to practice mutually. Sometimes I need to exercise this ministry to someone, but at other times, I will need him to exercise it towards me. This command assumes that you are having personal contact with other believers during the week and that they know what is going on in your life well enough to offer this ministry when you need it. Also, to exercise this service, you must realize that you *are* your brother's keeper! If you see your brother being hardened by the deceitfulness of sin, and you shrug it off, you are not obeying this command. You are responsible to help your brother who is struggling with unbelief or sin. You can't keep your distance.

> B. Encouragement is a service that is needed daily because the enemy attacks daily.

We are to do this "day after day." Don't assume, "Well, I'll let the pastor deal with him someday, but that's not my responsibility." It *is* your responsibility if you see your brother turning away from the Lord! Since Satan does not let up in his attacks, we must not let up on encouraging one another in the faith.

> C. Encouragement is a service that is needed because of the deceitfulness of sin.

A deceived person can't evaluate himself properly. He thinks that everything is fine when it's not fine. If you've ever been deceived by a con artist, he was long gone with your money before you realized that there was a problem. An outside party could have warned you, "Look out for that guy!" Maybe you would have avoided getting ripped off. Because sin fools us, we need one another to come alongside and give this ministry of encouragement.

To persevere, there is a great sin to avoid—unbelief. There is a great service to practice—encouragement.

3. To persevere in faith, there is a great salvation to hold fast to (3:14).

"For we have become partakers of Christ, if we hold fast the beginning of our assurance firm until the end." Two things:

> A. Salvation unites us to Christ.

"We have become partakers of Christ" (see also, 1:9; 3:1; 6:4; 12:8). Scholars are divided over whether this refers to our sharing with Christ in His kingdom work; or to our union with Christ, what Paul frequently calls being "in Christ." While both are true, the context seems to refer to our share in Christ Himself. When God saves us, He places us in Christ so that all that is true of Him is true of us. As Paul boldly states (Rom. 8:1), "Therefore there is now no condemnation for those who are in Christ Jesus."

> B. While final salvation for believers is certain, it is not automatic.

While "partakers of Christ" focuses on what God has done for us by grace, the "if" clause focuses on our responsibility. "The beginning of our assurance" refers to our initial faith in Christ for salvation. Saving faith isn't just a one-time action. If it is genuine, we go on believing until the time that we see Jesus ("the end"). It is our responsibility to hold fast to such faith and assurance.

In Philippians, Paul presents the same balance. He says that God will complete the good work that He began in us, but at the same time he exhorts us to work out our salvation, recognizing all the while that it is God who is at work in us (Phil. 1:6; 2:12-13). In other words, the promises about the certainty of our salvation should never cause us to kick back and assume that we have no responsibility in the process. Those who truly believe in Christ will continue to hold fast to faith in Him until the end. If they let go of their faith in Him, turn back to the world, and are content to stay there, it indicates that they never really trusted in Him as Savior at all. True believers may go through times of doubt and sin, but they can't remain there. God's discipline will bring them back (12:8).

To persevere in faith, there is a great sin to avoid, a great service to practice, and a great salvation to hold fast to. Finally,

4. To persevere in faith, there is a great story to personalize (3:15-19).

The author comes back to the story of Israel in the wilderness, quoting again from Psalm 95: "Today, if you hear His voice, do not harden your hearts, as when they provoked Me." Then he brings this story home to his readers by asking three sets of two rhetorical questions each (the KJV mistranslates 3:16). The first question in each set is answered by the second question. He wants his readers to see that their situation parallels exactly that of Israel in the wilderness. In 3:19 he sums up his point, tying it back to the idea of unbelief in 3:12.

The first question and answer (3:16) show that *this story applies to all professing believers*. "For who provoked Him when they had heard? Indeed, did not all those who came out of Egypt led by Moses?" While there was a truly saved remnant in that company, most of them grumbled, disbelieved God, and died in the wilderness. The author is saying to all professing Christians, "This applies to you!" Even if we are true believers, John Owen's comment is apropos

(*Hebrews: The Epistle of Warning* [Kregel], p. 53): "The best of saints have need to be cautioned against the worst of evils."

The second question and answer (3:17) show that *professing believers who persist in sin should expect God's anger, not His rest.* "And with whom was He angry for forty years? Was it not with those who sinned, whose bodies fell in the wilderness?" If we are not true believers, our sin in the face of knowledge will incur God's final judgment. If we are true believers, our sin will bring on His strong discipline. Either way, you don't want to go there!

The third question and answer (3:18) show that *those who incurred God's judgment in the wilderness were not only unbelieving; they were disobedient.* "And to whom did He swear that they would not enter His rest, but to those who were disobedient?" As we've seen, you cannot separate the two. Unbelief that is unchecked quickly moves into disobedience. Often unbelief is a smokescreen used to hide disobedience. Unbelief is more socially acceptable than sin, so we posture ourselves as struggling with intellectual issues. But beneath the surface, we know that if God's Word is true, then we need to turn from our sins, and we don't want to do that. The disobedient who failed to enter God's rest were one and the same with the unbelieving.

His final summary (3:19) also shows that unbelief renders us not only *unwilling*, but also *unable* to appropriate God's blessings: "So we see that they were not able to enter because of unbelief." Either faith opens the blessings of God's eternal rest to you, or unbelief bars you from them. To persevere in faith, we need to personalize the story of Israel in the wilderness. We need to avoid their awful sin of unbelief that rendered them unable to enter God's promised rest.

Conclusion

I had a neighbor in California who could be described as an all-out macho man. His face and tattooed arms were tanned from working on a road crew and from riding his motorcycle in the California sun. He had a quick temper. I once heard him from over 100 yards away cussing out the snowplow driver for plowing a berm in front of his driveway. He had copies of *Penthouse* magazine lying around his house. He never went to church.

One day I got an opportunity to share Christ with him. But he quickly held up his hand to silence me and then said, "Steve, I've got that all fixed up with the Man Upstairs." I'm always worried when someone refers to Almighty God as "the Man Upstairs." I asked, "What do you mean?" He proceeded to tell me that when he was a teenager, he attended a large Baptist church in the Los Angeles area. The youth pastor had told him that if he would accept Christ, he would be assured of going to heaven. He said, "I did that, and so you don't need to worry about me." Even though there was not a shred of evidence that he was persevering in the faith, and in spite of much evidence that he was not, he thought that because he had once believed, he had eternal life!

The author of Hebrews had a different view of things. He says that to enter God's rest, we must persevere in obedient faith. To persevere, we must avoid the great sin of unbelief; we must practice the great service of mutual encouragement; we must hold fast our great salvation in Christ; and, we must personalize the great story of Israel in the wilderness. Take care, brethren!

Application Questions

1. Why is unbelief such a terrible sin? Does this mean that true Christians never doubt? Why/why not?
2. Since sin is so deceptive, how can we recognize and deal with our unbelief? Is unbelief primarily intellectual or moral?
3. Should we share assurance of salvation with a person who says that he believes in Christ, but who is persisting in sin? What guidelines should we follow here?
4. Is the criticism valid, that if salvation entails perseverance, then we can never have assurance? Why/why not?

Hebrews 4:1-11, New American Standard Bible 1995

4:1: Therefore, let us fear if, while a promise remains of entering His rest, any one of you may seem to have come short of it. 2 For indeed we have had good news preached to us, just as they also; but the word they heard did not profit them, because it was not united by faith in those who heard. 3 For we who have believed enter that rest, just as He has said,

> "As I swore in My wrath,
> They shall not enter My rest,"

although His works were finished from the foundation of the world. 4 For He has said somewhere concerning the seventh day: "And God rested on the seventh day from all His works"; 5 and again in this passage, "They shall not enter My rest." 6 Therefore, since it remains for some to enter it, and those who formerly had good news preached to them failed to enter because of disobedience, 7 He again fixes a certain day, "Today," saying through David after so long a time just as has been said before,

> "Today if you hear His voice,
> Do not harden your hearts."

8 For if Joshua had given them rest, He would not have spoken of another day after that. 9 So there remains a Sabbath rest for the people of God. 10 For the one who has entered His rest has himself also rested from his works, as God did from His. 11 Therefore let us be diligent to enter that rest, so that no one will fall, through following the same example of disobedience.

Cultural Religion Versus Saving Faith
Hebrews 4:1-11

For me, some of the most frightening words in the Bible are Jesus' words in Matthew 7:21-23:

> "Not everyone who says to Me, 'Lord, Lord,' will enter the kingdom of heaven, but he who does the will of My Father who is in heaven *will enter*. Many will say to Me on that day, 'Lord, Lord, did we not prophesy in Your name, and in Your name cast out demons, and in Your name perform many miracles?' And then I will declare to them, 'I never knew you; DEPART FROM ME, YOU WHO PRACTICE LAWLESSNESS.'"

Clearly, Jesus is warning us that it is possible not only to claim to follow Him, but also to serve Him in some remarkable ways—prophesying, casting out demons, and performing miracles—and yet be excluded from heaven! Jesus was not talking about pagans, who spent their lives partying and disregarding God. These were men that had spent their lives serving Him, or so they thought. Their cry, "Lord, Lord," shows that they professed Jesus as their Lord. Clearly, they were shocked at being shut out of heaven. They expected to get in, but when they got there, the door was barred! If Jesus' words do not strike fear into your heart, they should!

Both Jesus' words and the words of our text warn us against the danger of cultural Christianity. Cultural Christians go to church. They claim to believe in Jesus as Savior and Lord. Many of them serve in the church. But on that great and terrible day, they will hear Jesus utter the chilling words, "I never knew you; depart from Me, you who practice lawlessness." I want to explain how to avoid being a cultural Christian and how to be genuinely saved.

Hebrews 4:1-11 is a difficult text to understand. While I think that I am on the right track here, I confess that for many years I could not understand these verses. Many pastors and Bible scholars apply these verses along the lines of how believers can experience God's peace or rest in the face of trials in our daily walk. I grant that there may be a valid *secondary* application in that sense.

But as I have wrestled with these verses in their context, I think that to apply them primarily as an encouragement to believers to rest in Christ in the midst of trials is to misapply them. Rather, I think that the main message is:

Cultural Religion Versus Saving Faith

All who are associated with the church must beware of the cultural religion that falls short of personally experiencing God's salvation.

In other words, I view these verses as a warning to professing Christians to make sure that their faith is genuine. I am going to follow the old Puritan approach to sermon structure, first explaining the doctrine and then giving "the use" (applying the text).

DOCTRINE: THE TEXT EXPLAINED IN ITS CONTEXT:

Two statements will help us understand the text:

1. **The author is not talking about an experience of inner calm that some believers may lack; rather, he is talking about experiencing God's salvation (Context).**

"Therefore" (4:1) takes us back to chapter 3, especially to verses 12 & 19. He is warning against having an evil, unbelieving heart. His readers were Jewish believers in Christ who were tempted in the face of persecution to go back to Judaism. Twice he exhorts them to "hold fast" their confession or assurance of faith (3:6, 14). He cited Psalm 95:7-11, which recounts how the Israelites in the wilderness provoked God and were thereby excluded from entering His place of rest, the Promised Land. They all had applied the blood of the Passover lamb to their doorposts. They all had passed through the Red Sea and escaped from Pharaoh's army. But even so, with most of them, God was not well pleased, and He laid them low in the wilderness (1 Cor. 10:5).

To understand that story correctly, it is important that we not push the typology too far. We would be mistaken to conclude that all of those who came out of Egypt were true believers who were "living in carnality." I have often heard the story applied in this way. Those in Israel who grumbled in the wilderness are likened to "carnal" Christians. They are saved, but they just haven't yet moved into Canaan's land, which is the experience of victory over sin. Sometimes this is phrased that they are still in Romans 7, but they haven't yet moved into Romans 8. I contend that that is to misapply this story.

Rather, I think that those who rebelled in the wilderness and incurred God's wrath represent what I am calling "cultural believers." They were a part of the people of God (Israel), but their hearts were far from trusting in the Lord. Their hearts are repeatedly described as hardened (3:8, 13, 15; 4:7). They were under God's wrath (3:10, 11, 17, 18; 4:3). Their basic problem is called unbelief (3:12; 4:2), disobedience, and sin (3:17, 18; 4:6, 11).

The author plainly is talking about a person's response to the gospel, not to an experience of a deeper Christian life. Twice he states that these people, like us, had the good news preached to them (4:2, 6). Even under the Law of Moses, people were not saved by keeping the Law, but by the righteousness of faith (Gen. 15:6; Exod. 34:6-7; Ps. 32:1-2; cf. Rom. 4). But the good news did not benefit these people, because it was not united with faith (4:2).

Thus when the author exhorts us to fear, lest we may come short of entering God's rest (4:1), the thing we are to fear is unbelief and its terrible consequences, namely, eternal judgment. We should fear that like these grumbling unbelievers, we may fall through the same example of disobedience (4:11; cf. 3:17). Either we have entered God's rest (His salvation) through faith, or we are the objects of His wrath through unbelief and disobedience (3:10-11, 16-18; 4:3, 5). If we do not believe God's promises, those very promises turn into frightening threats of judgment!

So I contend that the context shows us that the author's pastoral concern was not that some "carnal" Christians in the Hebrew church would miss out on the experience of God's peace in the midst of their trials. His main concern was that some of them may be like those in Israel in the wilderness. They may be a part of the religious crowd, but not true believers. His concern was for their salvation from God's wrath through genuine saving faith.

A second statement will help us understand our text:

2. God always has offered His salvation to people, and still offers it, under the imagery of rest (4:3-10).

The train of thought in 4:3-10 is difficult, but I think that the author is explaining from the Old Testament how the imagery of God's rest has been a picture of salvation in four different time periods.

A. At creation, God's rest on the seventh day was a picture of the rest that we enjoy in Him (4:3-4).

The author begins by stating, "For we who believe enter that rest." Then he cites again Psalm 95:11, "As I swore in My wrath, they shall not enter My rest" (see Heb. 3:11). Then he adds, "although His works were finished from the foundation of the world." He goes on to cite from Genesis 2:2, how "God rested on the seventh day from all His works." F. F. Bruce (*Commentary on the Epistle to the Hebrews* [Eerdmans], p. 74) explains the thought connection: "It was not because the 'rest' of God was not yet available that the wilderness generation of Israelites failed to enter into it; it had been available ever since creation's work was ended."

In other words, the Jewish Sabbath, which was rooted in the creation narrative, was a picture of the rest that God's people enjoy through His salvation. It was a day to cease from normal labors and to be refreshed through time with God. It was a weekly opportunity for God's people to stop and reflect on His goodness and care for them. From the beginning, there was a spiritual element to the Sabbath. The soul in harmony with his creator found a sense of satisfaction and rest on that day.

    B. At Canaan, the Promised Land was a picture of the rest that God offers through faith in Him (4:5, 8).

The author repeats (see 4:3) the last phrase of Psalm 95:11, "They shall not enter My rest," to refer to the generation that perished in the wilderness. In 4:8 he shows that even those who entered the Promised Land under Joshua did not experience the fullness of God's rest, in that David, over 300 years after Joshua, spoke of the need to enter God's rest. In the Greek text, Joshua is *Iesous*, "Jesus," which means, "Yahweh saves." So the original readers would have seen the play on the names: the original Jesus (Joshua) was only a type of the Jesus to come. Joshua led the people into the Promised Land, but that was only a picture of the rest of God's salvation that Jesus Christ provides.

    C. Canaan was not God's final rest, since David wrote of a rest available to God's people in his day (4:6-7).

Since those in the wilderness failed to enter God's rest, and since David wrote, "Today, if you hear His voice, do not harden your hearts," there is still a day of opportunity to respond to God's offer of rest. The emphasis here is on the word "today." The gist of the argument here is that God's promises always have a present application to them. Even though Israel in the wilderness failed to appropriate God's rest, God offered it again through David. Every generation has the opportunity to respond in faith to God's promises. This leads to the bottom line:

D. God is still appealing to us to enter His rest through faith (4:9-10).

The author here uses a unique word for rest, translated "Sabbath rest." Some think that he coined the word. It calls attention to the spiritual aspect of God's rest. It goes beyond observing the seventh day as holy. It goes beyond entering the physical Promised Land. This Sabbath rest is a soul-rest. It is what Jesus promised when He said (Matt. 11:28-30),

> "Come to Me, all who are weary and heavy-laden, and I will give you rest. Take My yoke upon you and learn from Me, for I am gentle and humble in heart, and YOU WILL FIND REST FOR YOUR SOULS. For My yoke is easy and My burden is light."

The author says that this rest remains for "the people of God" (4:9). Then he explains that "the one who has entered His rest has himself also rested from his works, as God did from His" (4:10). "The people of God" refers to Israel in the Old Testament, and here to all who are associated with God's church. Bruce (p. 78) thinks that verses 9-10 refer to "an experience which they do not enjoy in their present mortal life, although it belongs to them as a heritage, and by faith they may live in the good of it here and now." He refers to the believers in chapter 11, who did not experience the fullness of the promises in their lifetimes, but who were looking for the heavenly city that God prepared for them (11:16).

Leon Morris (*Expositor's Bible Commentary*, ed. by Frank Gaebelein [Zondervan], 12:43) cites Bruce and then comments,

> I should reverse his order and say that they live in it here and now by faith, but what they know here is not the full story. That will be revealed in the hereafter. There is a sense in which to enter Christian salvation means to cease from one's works and rest securely on what Christ has done.

The author's point here is that from the beginning God has offered His salvation to people, and still offers it, under this imagery of entering His rest. At the heart of it is that we stop trusting in our works to save us and begin trusting instead in the finished work of Christ to save us. As Paul puts it (Rom.

4:5), "to the one who does not work, but believes in Him who justifies the ungodly, his faith is credited as righteousness."

To sum up, when the author talks of entering God's rest, he is not talking about believers learning to trust God in trials so that they experience His inner peace. Rather, he is talking about God's salvation under the imagery of rest, in line with the Old Testament. He is warning his readers about the danger of being associated with God's people but missing His salvation because they do not respond in faith to the message.

USE: THE TEXT APPLIED TO US:

I offer seven applications. Some of these are repeated from earlier chapters, but since the writer hammers these things home through repetition, so will I.

1. Cultural religion (general belief) will save no one; to be saved, we must have personal faith in Jesus Christ.

The Jews in the wilderness believed in God in a general sense. They knew and believed in the story of creation and the history recorded in Genesis. They believed that the covenant with Abraham applied to them as his descendants. They even believed God enough to apply the blood to their doorposts and to follow Moses through the Red Sea. They had heard God's good news, but it did not profit them because they did not believe it personally (4:2). When they heard about the giants in the land, they complained that it would have been better to die in Egypt or to die in the wilderness than to be killed by the Canaanites (Num. 14:2-3). So God granted them their wish; they all died in the wilderness!

It is not enough to grow up in the church and have a general belief in God and in Jesus Christ. Perhaps you've heard the gospel all your life, and intellectually, you believe in Jesus and that He died for your sins. But intellectual belief is not enough! Saving faith trusts personally in the shed blood of Jesus as the only payment for *my* sins. Saving faith believes that God will be gracious *to me* in the judgment because *my* sins are covered by Jesus' blood and that His righteousness has been imputed *to me* according to God's promise. Make sure that your hope of heaven is not based on your parents' faith or on the fact that you hang out with Christians in a church building! You must see your need as a sinner before God and come personally to Christ in faith to receive God's mercy.

2. **Beware of the false peace that comes through cultural religion.**

   I fear that there are many in our churches today, like those Jesus referred to, who will say, "Lord, Lord," but who will be shut out of heaven. Jeremiah 6:14 warned about false prophets, who healed the brokenness of God's people superficially, saying, "Peace, peace," but there is no peace. People today are encouraged to "invite Jesus into their hearts" and then are told that they have eternal life and will never lose it. They are not told that they need to repent of their sins. They are not told that God must change their hearts. Polls show that there is virtually no difference today between the way that "evangelicals" think and live and the way the rest of the population thinks and lives!

   Just because a person *feels* inner peace does not mean that he is truly saved. I encourage you to read Jonathan Edwards' *A Treatise on Religious Affections* (a modern English, condensed version is called, *The Experience that Counts*). He analyzes in great detail, with an abundance of Scriptural support, how a person can know which feelings are valid indicators of genuine conversion.

3. **Saving faith is a matter of the heart towards God, not of outward religion.**

   Verse 7 is the third time the author has repeated the warning not to harden our hearts (3:8, 15). God looks on the heart, not on the outward performance of religious duties. Salvation is a matter of God doing "heart surgery," replacing our hearts of stone with hearts of flesh (Ezek. 36:26) that are tender towards Him. If you are truly saved, you know that your heart is different than it was before. It is not that you never sin now, but rather that your attitude towards sin is radically different. Before, you loved it; now, you hate it. Before, you were apathetic towards the things of God. Now, you love God and His Word. The bent of your life is a desire to know Him and love Him more and more.

4. **Saving faith is always obedient faith.**

   As we saw in the last chapter, the author uses faith and obedience (or, unbelief and disobedience) interchangeably (3:18-19; 4:2, 6, 11). It is not that we are saved by works, but rather that true saving faith *always* results in a life of obedience to God. Again, I'm not talking about sinless perfection. No one lives perfectly this side of heaven. But a true believer strives against sin (Heb. 12:4). Instead of being a slave of sin, a believer is a slave of righteousness out of obedience from the heart (Rom. 6:17-18). A person who is not growing in obedience to God's Word should question whether his faith is genuine saving faith, or just cultural religion.

5. Saving faith rests completely on the work of Jesus Christ.

If we are depending on anything in ourselves to get into heaven, we have not entered God's rest (4:10). It is possible even to depend wrongly on your faith, thinking that your faith gets you into heaven. To do this is to turn faith into a work! It becomes the thing you are trusting for eternal life. Don't trust in your faith; trust in Christ. If salvation were based on my faith, then it would be due to something in me, and not according to grace (Rom. 11:6). God saves us by His grace, based on the merit of Jesus Christ. Faith simply looks to Christ and relies on Him alone.

6. Saving faith is effortless in one sense, but requires diligent perseverance in another sense.

There is a sense of irony in the exhortation (4:11), "Let us be diligent to enter that rest." While salvation is a gift that we passively receive, there is also an active responsibility on our part to lay hold of it. We must rest from our works (4:10), but be diligent to enter God's true rest (4:11). As I said in the last chapter, you can cruise into hell without any effort. Just go with the flow of the world, the flesh, and the devil, and you'll get there. But getting into heaven requires diligence and watchfulness. Jesus said (Luke 13:24), "Strive to enter through the narrow door; for many, I tell you, will seek to enter and will not be able." Be diligent in seeking God's rest through His Word, so that you do not come short of it.

7. Saving faith results in great confidence in God in present trials and great hope in God for future eternal joy.

The rest spoken of here is both a present reality and a future hope. The present reality is, as Paul said (Rom. 5:1), "having been justified by faith, we have peace with God through our Lord Jesus Christ." It also includes, as he goes on to say (Rom. 5:3-5), that "we also exult in our tribulations, knowing that tribulation brings about perseverance; and perseverance, proven character; and proven character, hope; and hope does not disappoint, because the love of God has been poured out within our hearts through the Holy Spirit who was given to us." The future hope is the promise of being with the Lord forever in glory, when "He will wipe away every tear from [our] eyes; and there will no longer be any mourning, or crying, or pain" (Rev. 21:4).

Conclusion

I hope that this chapter has disturbed the comfortable and comforted the disturbed. If you began reading feeling comfortable in your standing before God because you are associated with a church, or because you serve in some way in the church, or because of anything you do, I hope you are now disturbed because you see that your standing with God is on shaky ground. To base your hope for heaven on any outward religion is to have false hope.

On the other hand, if you began reading feeling disturbed because you were despairing of your propensity toward sin, and you knew that if salvation depended on your performance, you would never qualify, I hope that you are comforted with the good news that you can enter God's eternal rest through faith in Christ alone. Fear the unbelief of cultural Christianity! Trust in the Savior who gives true rest to His people!

Application Questions

1. Do you agree with the interpretation offered? Why/why not?
2. Do doubts mean that our faith is not genuine? How can we know if our faith is genuine?
3. What are some marks of cultural religion versus true faith?
4. How can fear (4:1) abide with true faith? See Luke 12:5; Rom. 11:20; Phil. 2:13.

Hebrews 4:12-13, New American Standard Bible 1995

12 For the word of God is living and active and sharper than any two-edged sword, and piercing as far as the division of soul and spirit, of both joints and marrow, and able to judge the thoughts and intentions of the heart. 13 And there is no creature hidden from His sight, but all things are open and laid bare to the eyes of Him with whom we have to do.

God's Powerful Word
Hebrews 4:12-13

Expository preaching has fallen on hard times. Many are saying that people who are used to television and other modern media cannot handle a 40-minute sermon. Sadly, many pastors are heeding that advice. "Seeker" churches advocate 15-minute talks built around some felt need, accompanied by short dramas to hold people's attention. They say that we should never mention sin or anything else that will make anyone feel uncomfortable! The aim is to make everyone feel good in church.

That approach to ministry is an inherent denial of the power of God's Word to convert sinners and build up God's people by exposing our sin and pointing to God's grace at the cross. History contains numerous testimonies to the power of God's Word. A guilt-ridden monk named Martin Luther got saved by studying Romans 1:16-17. When people praised Luther for his role in the Reformation, he deflected the praise to the Word. He said (in Eric Gritsch, *Martin—God's Court Jester* [Fortress Press], pp. 200-201),

> "And while I slept, or drank Wittenberg beer with my friends Philip [Melanchthon] and [Nicholas] Amsdorf, the Word so greatly weakened the papacy that no prince or emperor ever inflicted such losses upon it. I did nothing; the Word did everything."

In a similar manner, God brought the Reformation to Geneva through the biblical preaching of John Calvin. In *Calvin's Preaching* [Westminster/John Knox Press], T. H. L. Parker shows the amazing expository ministry that Calvin carried out in Geneva. He would normally preach two different sermons on Sundays, and then different sermons each weekday on alternate weeks. His sermons normally lasted one hour. The weeks that he didn't preach at the church, he was teaching ministerial students at the seminary. In addition to his heavy preaching load, he met weekly with the church leaders, visited the sick, counseled those in need, maintained an extensive correspondence, and wrote his many commentaries and books (pp. 62-63)! Think what he could have done with a computer or if he hadn't died at age 54!

I have read several books of Calvin's sermons. His style is to explain the text in simple terms that ordinary people could understand, even though he preached directly out of his Hebrew and Greek Testaments, without notes. After Easter Sunday, 1538, the town fathers banished Calvin from Geneva. They later realized their mistake, and brought him back in September 1541. Calvin picked up with the next verse after the one he had taught in 1538, as if it had been the previous Sunday (p. 60)! His theme invariably was to show God's majesty and holiness, our wretchedness and spiritual poverty, and the riches of grace that God in His fatherly kindness has made available to us through Christ (pp. 93-107).

Hebrews 4:12-13 is one of the great biblical texts on the power of God's Word. The author has been warning the Hebrew church of the danger of cultural Christianity. His text has been Psalm 95, which refers to the tragic example of Israel in the wilderness. Although they had come out of Egypt by applying the Passover blood, had come through the Red Sea, and had been sustained in the wilderness by God's provision of water and manna, they did not trust God or obey His Word. As a result, they failed to enter God's rest, which was a picture of salvation.

In verse 11 the author warns, "let us be diligent to enter that rest, so that no one will fall, through following the same example of disobedience." Verse 12 begins with "For." The connection is that Israel in the wilderness had God's Word, but disregarded it. We should not follow their example of disobedience to the Word. It will do a powerful work in our hearts if we hear it, allow it to expose our sin, and obey it. Since God sees and knows everything, including our very thoughts, we would be fools to disobey His life-giving Word. To do so would only bring certain judgment. Thus,

Because God's Word is powerful to expose our sin and God Himself sees everything, we must be diligent to have our hearts right before Him.

Many early commentators interpreted "the word" here to refer to Jesus Christ, whom John (1:1) calls "the Word." Granted, the author begins Hebrews by stating, "God, after He spoke long ago to the fathers in the prophets in many portions and in many ways, in these last days has spoken to us in His Son" (1:1-2). But in the immediate context, he has been showing how Israel in the wilderness did not hear (in the sense of obey) God's voice (3:7, 15; 4:7).

They had the good news preached to them, but they did not unite it with faith and obedience (4:2, 6).

In this context, "the word of God" refers to all of God's spoken revelation, including that which came through His Son. We have it recorded in written form in the Scriptures. If we heed God's Word, it will keep us from the cultural religion that brings sure judgment. The author is extolling the power of God's Word to bring us into a personal experience of His rest, or salvation.

1. God's Word is powerful to expose our sin (4:12).

The text asserts four things about the power of the Word:

A. God's Word is living.

Since God is the living God (3:12), and His Word cannot be separated from Him, that Word is a living Word. It can never be exterminated. As Isaiah 40:8 proclaims, "The grass withers, the flower fades, but the word of our God stands forever." Since God is the author of life, His living Word imparts life in two ways.

1) God's Word imparts new life to dead sinners.

Because of sin, we all enter this world dead in trespasses and sins, alienated from God (Eph. 2:1, 12). A dead sinner cannot will himself into spiritual life any more than a dead corpse can will himself into physical life. But God is pleased to use His Word to impart new life to dead sinners. James 1:18 states, "In the exercise of His will [not *our* will] He brought us forth by the word of truth ..." 1 Peter 1:23 says, "for you have been born again not of seed which is perishable but imperishable, that is, through the living and enduring word of God."

If you want to see sinners converted, get them to read and listen to God's Word. John (20:31) stated very plainly his purpose in writing his gospel: "these [signs] have been written so that you may believe that Jesus is the Christ, the Son of God; and that believing you may have life in His name."

Many years ago, Marla's sister, Sandie, was living a godless life. In her words, she was "living with her boyfriend, drinking, smoking, and cussing." One of the first times we were together, I asked her when she was going to become a Christian. She sputtered, "Probably never!" I asked, "Why not?" She said, "Because I don't believe the Bible." I asked, "Have you ever read it carefully?" I pointed out that Marla and I were both reasonably intelligent people, and we believed the Bible. Finally, after months of pestering, she agreed to read the Bible. She ended up reading it cover to cover in two months and became a Christian. I had the joy of baptizing her.

When I emailed to ask if I could use her story she said, "Yes you may definitely use my story. I still thank you and Marla for not giving up on me. If it had not been for your persistence and getting the word of God into my hands, I would probably be dead and in hell today because of my sinful lifestyle in those days. And you can quote me."

2) God's Word imparts renewed life to His saints.

All of us that have known God's salvation for a while have gone through dry times when God seemed distant. God uses His Word to renew and revive us. David wrote (Ps. 19:7), "The law of the Lord is perfect, restoring the soul." The entire 176 verses of Psalm 119 extol the benefits of God's Word. Repeatedly the psalmist cries out (119:25), "My soul cleaves to the dust; revive me according to Your word." Psalm 119:50: "This is my comfort in my affliction, that Your word has revived me" (see also, verses 93, 107, 149, 154, 156, 159).

It only makes sense that if the living God, has spoken to us in His written Word, then we should seek it like a treasure and devour it as a hungry man devours a meal. Being the word *of God*, it is both a word *from* God and a word *about* God. It is our only source of knowing specific truth about God. Creation reveals His attributes in a general way, but the written Word is God's disclosure of Himself in a way that we could never know through creation alone. And invariably, when we see God as He is, we also see ourselves as we are, as Isaiah experienced (Isa. 6:1-5). While this shatters us at first, it is always for our ultimate healing and growth in holiness.

As the living Word, God's revelation also speaks to our current needs and situation. As we have seen, the author often quotes Scripture by saying, "He says" (1:5; 2:11-12), or "The Holy Spirit says" (3:7). Even though the Bible was written many centuries ago, the Spirit of God still speaks directly to us through it. It is never out of date or irrelevant. It speaks to the very issues that we face in our modern world. I would encourage you to read the Bible not in a random manner, but consecutively, from both the Old and New Testaments. You will find, as I have, that God will often use what you have read either that day or within a few days of reading it.

B. God's Word is active.

We get our word "energy" from the Greek word translated "active." It means that the Word is effectual. It accomplishes what God intends for it to do. As Isaiah 55:10-11 states, "For as the rain and the snow come down from heaven, and do not return there without watering the earth and making it bear and sprout, and furnishing seed to the sower and bread to the eater; so will My word be which goes forth out of My mouth; it will not return to Me empty, without accomplishing what I desire, and without succeeding in the matter for which I sent it." I claim that verse every time I preach! If I am careful to preach God's Word, and not my own, He promises that *it will* accomplish His purpose.

You may wonder, "What about people who hear and reject God's Word?" Jesus explained that these people are only fulfilling another word from God to Isaiah (Matt. 13:14-15, citing Isa. 6:9-10),

"You will keep on hearing, but will not understand; you will keep on seeing, but will not perceive; for the heart of this people has become dull, with their ears they scarcely hear, and they have closed their eyes. Otherwise they would see with their eyes, hear with their ears, and understand with their heart and return, and I would heal them."

As John Owen explains (*Hebrews: The Epistle of Warning* [Kregel abridgement], p. 74), "Sometimes Christ designs by His word the hardening and blinding of wicked sinners, that they may be the more prepared for deserved destruction."

In my first year at Flagstaff Christian Fellowship, I was preaching through 1 Peter and came to chapter 3, where he instructs wives to be submissive to their husbands, even if the husbands are disobedient to the word. That week, a single woman in her 30's came to see me. She said, "You should never preach on that on a Sunday morning." I asked her if I had misrepresented what the text says. She replied, "No, you taught what it says." I asked, "Did I say it in an arrogant or condescending manner?" She replied, "No, you had the proper tone of voice and manner of speaking."

So I asked, "Then what was the problem?" She said, "The problem was, I brought a friend with me who is an ardent feminist. She was offended and will never come to church again!" I said, "Ah! Well, I've been doing this for a few years now, and I know that one of two things will happen. Either your friend will be convicted of her rebellion against God and come to repentance. Or, she will harden her heart and be all the more guilty on the day of judgment. But either way, God's Word will not return to Him void, without accomplishing His purpose." The woman didn't like my answer and left the church.

C. God's Word is sharp and piercing.

It is "sharper than any two-edged sword, and piercing as far as the division of soul and spirit, of both joints and marrow..." Some use this verse to draw distinctions between soul and spirit, but that is not the author's intent. (What then would the distinction between joints and marrow mean?) Rather, he is using figurative language to show that God's Word is sharp and it cuts deeply, to the very core of our being. Unless your conscience is hardened beyond remedy, you cannot read God's Word or hear it preached faithfully without getting cut in the conscience.

God's purpose in cutting us is to bring healing, not to leave us wounded. Sin is like a cancer growing inside of us. Untreated, it will be fatal. The sharp sword of God's Word, as J. B. Lightfoot put it (*Cambridge Sermons* [Macmillan and Co.], p. 162), "heals most completely, where it wounds most deeply; and gives life there only, where first it has killed." David Livingstone, the pioneer missionary to Africa, offered to teach one of the chiefs to shoot a rifle and also to read. But the chief replied that "he did not wish to learn to read the Book, for he was afraid it might change his heart and make him content with only one wife, like Sechele" (another chief who had been converted) (George Seaver, *David Livingstone: His Life and Letters* [Harper & Brothers], p. 177). He wanted to get five wives before he dared to read the Bible!

The Bible is a dangerous book! It will cut you! When it makes your conscience go, "Ow!" don't harden your heart. Let God do surgery by cutting out the cancer of sin that the Word has revealed.

D. God's Word is an authoritative judge of the thoughts and intentions of the heart.

The word "thoughts" refers to negative thoughts related to emotions, such as anger, which a man may wish to keep hidden from others, but which God knows (B. F. Westcott, *The Epistle to the Hebrews* [Eerdmans], p. 103; H. Schonweiss, in *The New International Dictionary of New Testament Theology*, ed. by Colin Brown, 1:106). "Intentions" refers here to "morally questionable thoughts" (*Theological Dictionary of the New Testament*, ed. by Gerhard Kittel, 4:971). The heart refers to the totality of the inner person. We get our word "critic" from the word translated "judge." So the idea is that God's Word is able authoritatively to act as critic of our innermost feelings and thoughts, showing us where we are wrong.

I've had the experience after I've preached of a husband coming to me, looking around to make sure that no one is listening, and asking nervously, "Did my wife talk to you about what went on in our household this week?" I chuckle and assure him, "No, I had no idea what was going on, but God did!" His Word penetrated into the secrecy of that home and heart, revealing things that were not in line with His righteousness.

So in verse 12, the author is showing how God's Word is powerful to expose our sin, never for the purpose of embarrassing us, but always to bring healing. We cannot rid our lives of sin if we aren't even aware of it. The Word cuts down to our inner thoughts and feelings, revealing to us the things that are not pleasing to God, so that we can repent of these things and receive God's restoration.

2. God Himself sees everything, including our deepest thoughts and motives (4:13).

The author moves from God's penetrating Word to God Himself, who sees everything. It is impossible to hide from God! Adam and Eve tried to hide from God after they sinned, but they could not do it, and neither can we. The word "open" means "naked." Have you ever dreamed that you were naked in public? What a relief after a dream like that, to wake up and realize that it was only a dream! But we stand naked *on the inside* before God!

"Laid bare" is used only here in the New Testament, and rarely anywhere else. It means to expose the neck, perhaps as a sacrificial victim's neck is exposed just before the knife slices the jugular vein. The idea of the two words together is that we are naked and helpless before God. There is no escape from His omniscient gaze. Sin is always stupid, because even if we fool everyone on earth, and think that we got away with it, we didn't fool God!

3. Since we all will give account to God, we must be diligent to have our hearts right before Him.

The final phrase of 4:13 means either "Him with whom we have to do," or, "Him to whom we must give an account." We know that one day we all will stand before God to give an account of the deeds we have done in this body. Therefore, we should have as our ambition to be pleasing to Him (2 Cor. 5:9-10), not just outwardly, but on the heart level.

If that thought terrifies you, keep reading! The author will go on to show how Jesus is our sympathetic High Priest who invites us to draw near to the throne of grace to receive mercy and grace to help in our time of need (4:14-16). But you must make sure that He truly is *your* High Priest, in the most personal sense. There is no group plan of salvation. It's not enough to be a part of the company of God's people. We must be diligent *personally* to enter God's rest through faith in Christ and obedience to His Word. Every true believer will develop the habit of judging sin on the thought or heart level, out of a desire to please the Savior who gave Himself for us on the cross.

Conclusion

I close with five practical action steps:

(1) Treasure God's Word above all worldly counsel! I am amazed at how Christians will pay psychologists hundreds of dollars for advice that is devoid of God's Word, but they won't consult the Bible for wisdom on how to live! You say, "But I needed advice on some practical relational problems." Why do you think the Bible was written? The whole thing is summed up by, "Love the Lord your God and love your neighbor." That's pretty relational! It's not only sin to neglect God's Word and turn to the empty "wisdom" of the world (Jer. 2:13). It's also just plain dumb!

(2) Read, study, memorize, and meditate on God's Word. It will not do you any good if you don't know what it says. You need to memorize key verses because you will not obey it if it's not in your heart (Ps. 119:11). You won't stop at work or at home to say, "Just a minute, I know there's a verse that applies here, but I need to get out my concordance and find it!"

(3) Apply, trust, and obey God's Word. The point of Bible study is not to fill your head with knowledge about the end times or theological arguments to support your favorite views. It is to change your heart and life! Always study it with a view to obedience.

(4) Live with your heart exposed to God's Word. Don't cover up any sinful thoughts. If the Word convicts you, stop and confess the matter to God. If need be, resolve to go to anyone you have wronged and ask forgiveness. Remember, God knows every sinful thought you'll ever have, and He still sent His Son to bear the penalty of your sin!

(5) Drink in all of the biblical preaching you can absorb. Don't get sucked in to the "preaching lite" movement! Calvin commented on verse 12 (*Calvin's Commentaries* [Baker], 22:102), "If anyone thinks that the air is beaten by an empty sound when the Word of God is preached, he is greatly mistaken; for it is a living thing and full of hidden power, which leaves nothing in man untouched." Be diligent to saturate yourself with God's Word with the aim of obedience, so that you do not fall as the stubborn Israelites did in the wilderness!

Application Questions

1. Since we know that sin destroys us, why do we persist in covering it up, rather than exposing it so that God can heal us?

2. Why is the "seeker" church movement inherently flawed?

3. What principles underlie sound biblical application?

4. In one sense, the Pharisees "knew" the Word. Why didn't it profit them? How can we avoid their mistakes?

Hebrews 4:14-16, New American Standard Bible 1995

14 Therefore, since we have a great high priest who has passed through the heavens, Jesus the Son of God, let us hold fast our confession. 15 For we do not have a high priest who cannot sympathize with our weaknesses, but One who has been tempted in all things as we are, yet without sin. 16 Therefore let us draw near with confidence to the throne of grace, so that we may receive mercy and find grace to help in time of need.

The Throne of Grace
Hebrews 4:14-16

All Christians struggle with two crucial areas that will make or break us in the Christian life: perseverance in times of trial; and, prayer. As you know, they are connected. A vital prayer life is essential to endure trials.

Failure to endure trials is the mark of the seed sown on rocky soil. Jesus explained (Mark 4:17) that this seed represents those who, "when they hear the word, immediately receive it with joy; and they have no firm root in themselves, but are only temporary; then, when affliction or persecution arises because of the word, immediately they fall away." Endurance is one mark of genuine saving faith (Heb. 3:6).

Prayer is our supply line to God in the battle. His abundant, sustaining grace flows to us through prayer. Because prayer is so vital, the enemy tries to sever that supply line. When we suffer, the enemy often whispers, "God doesn't care about you and He isn't answering. Why waste your time with these worthless prayers?" It's easy to get discouraged and quit praying, which cuts us off from the very help that we need!

Our text is one of the most encouraging passages in the Bible when it comes to perseverance and prayer. The first readers of this epistle were tempted to abandon their Christian faith and return to Judaism because of persecution. The author has just given an extended exhortation, using the bad example of Israel in the wilderness. They failed to enter God's rest (a picture of salvation) because of unbelief and disobedience. Therefore, we must be diligent to enter that rest. If we will respond in faith and obedience to God's Word, it will expose our sin and show us His ways. It is foolish to think that we can hide our sin from God, because everything is naked and laid bare in His sight (4:12-13).

Martin Luther commented on our text (in Philip Hughes, *Commentary on the Epistle to the Hebrews* [Eerdmans], p. 169), "After terrifying us, the Apostle now comforts us; after pouring wine into our wound, he now pours in oil." Rather than trying to hide because of our sin, the author shows how we should draw near to Jesus, our sympathetic high priest, who gives us access to God's throne. For those who are in Christ, that throne is not a place of fear but, rather, a throne of grace!

The Throne of Grace

Since Jesus is our great sympathetic high priest, we must persevere and we must pray.

There are two commands here: Hold fast our confession (persevere; 4:14); and, Draw near with confidence (pray; 4:16). They are both based on the truth about who Jesus is: Since Jesus is our great high priest, the Son of God, who has passed through the heavens, we must hold fast our confession. And, since Jesus is a high priest who sympathizes with our weaknesses, we should draw near to the throne of grace for help in our times of need. Thus His transcendence to the right hand of God's throne and His humanity are both essential elements of His unique effectiveness as our high priest. If we want to persevere through trials and receive His help through prayer, we must understand who He is.

1. **Since Jesus is our great high priest who has passed through the heavens, we must persevere (4:14).**

The author tells us who Jesus is and how we should respond.

A. Jesus is our great high priest who has passed through the heavens.

We see Jesus' greatness in two ways here:

    1) Jesus is great in His office as high priest at the right hand of God.

We have difficulty relating to the concept of a high priest, but to the Jews, it was an important office. Moses' brother Aaron was the first high priest. He was the mediator between the people and God. He and his fellow priests offered the sacrifices on behalf of the people. They had to follow a detailed procedure spelled out by God. Any variance or innovation meant instant death, as Aaron's two sons, Nadab and Abihu discovered when they offered "strange fire" on the altar (Lev. 10:1-3).

Once a year, on the Day of Atonement, the high priest alone would go into the Holy of Holies to make atonement for all the sins of the nation. If he entered there improperly or at any other time, he would die (Leviticus 16). He would sprinkle the blood on the mercy seat in the very presence of God. When he came out alive, the people heaved a sigh of relief, because it meant that God had accepted the sacrifice for their sins for another year.

Jesus is not just another high priest in the line of Aaron. Rather, He is our great high priest according to the order of Melchizedek (5:6). Rather than entering the Holy of Holies in the temple, He has passed through the heavens (in His ascension) into the very presence of God. The Jews thought of the sky as the first heaven. The stars are the second heaven. The presence of God is the third heaven (2 Cor. 12:2). Whether the author has this in mind or is just using "heavens" in the plural because the Hebrew word is always plural, we cannot say for certain.

But his point is that Jesus, our great high priest, is unlike any merely human high priest. He has entered the very presence of God. The Father has said to Him (Ps. 110:1), "Sit at My right hand until I make Your enemies a footstool for your feet." No earthly priest would dare to *sit* in the Holy of Holies! They always stood. But Jesus *sits* at the right hand of God's throne because once for all He made atonement for our sins (Heb. 10:12). So Jesus is a great high priest, in a class by Himself because of His office as a priest forever according to the order of Melchizedek (which the author will explain more in the following chapters).

2) Jesus is great in His Person as God in human flesh.

"Jesus" is His human name, calling attention to the full humanity of the Savior (see 2:17). If He had not been fully human, He could not have atoned for our sins. But He is also "the Son of God," which refers to His deity (John 5:18). As Bishop Moule said, "A Savior not quite God is a bridge broken at the farther end." Our author has shown in chapter 1 that Jesus is fully God. Thus Jesus is uniquely great in His office as high priest, and He is uniquely great in His person as God in human flesh. Therefore…

B. We must persevere.

The words, "hold fast our confession," imply danger and effort on our part (B. F. Westcott, *The Epistle to the Hebrews* [Eerdmans], p. 106). Picture someone hanging on for dear life as their raft goes down the raging rapids in the Grand Canyon. "Hold fast!" "Confession" implies not only our private belief in the essential doctrines of the faith (especially with regard to Jesus' deity and humanity), but also our public declaration of this truth in the face of persecution. We make such a public profession of faith in baptism, but that profession is put to the test when persecution arises. Are we only fair-weather believers who deny the Lord when it becomes costly to believe, or will we stand firm even to death because we know whom we have believed?

J. C. Ryle reports (*Home Truths* [Triangle Press], 1:64), "When John Rogers, the first martyr in Queen Mary's time, was being led to Smithfield to be burned, the French Ambassador reported that he looked as bright and cheerful as if he were going to his wedding." While God must give special grace at such a time, we would not do well in persecution if we grumble and walk away from God when we face lesser trials. Paul says that we're not only to persevere in trials, but to do so with great joy (Rom. 5:3)! So hold fast your confession of faith in Christ when He takes you through difficult trials. He is none other than your great high priest, God in human flesh, who now sits "at the right hand of the Majesty on high" (Heb. 1:3).

2. Since Jesus is our sympathetic and sinless high priest, we must pray in times of need (4:15-16).

A. Jesus is our sympathetic high priest.

The author uses a double negative, "We do not have a high priest who cannot sympathize with our weaknesses...." Probably he was anticipating an objection: "You've just said that Jesus is a great high priest who has passed through the heavens. How can someone beyond the heavens relate to me and my problems?" The author responds, "No, Jesus is not unsympathetic. He understands your deepest feelings."

We all need someone to sympathize with our problems and weaknesses without condemning us. Sometimes that is enough to get us through, just to know that someone else understands what we're going through. I read about a boy who noticed a sign, "Puppies for sale." He asked, "How much do you want for the pups, mister?"

"Twenty-five dollars, son." The boy's face dropped. "Well, sir, could I see them anyway?"

The man whistled and the mother dog came around the corner, followed by four cute puppies, wagging their tails and yipping happily. Then lagging behind, another puppy came around the corner, dragging one hind leg.

"What's the matter with that one, sir?" the boy asked.

"Well, son, that puppy is crippled. The vet took an X-ray and found that it doesn't have a hip socket. It will never be right."

The man was surprised when the boy said, "That's the one I want. Could I pay you a little each week?"

The owner replied, "But, son, you don't seem to understand. That pup will never be able to run or even walk right. He's going to be a cripple forever. Why would you want a pup like that?"

The boy reached down and pulled up his pant leg, revealing a brace. "I don't walk too good, either." Looking down at the puppy, the boy continued, "That puppy is going to need a lot of love and understanding. It's not easy being crippled!" The man said, "You can have the puppy for free. I know you'll take good care of him."

That is a limited illustration of our Savior's sympathy for our condition. Since He became a man and suffered all that we experience, He sympathizes with our weaknesses. He demonstrated His compassion many times during His earthly ministry. But His humanity was not diminished in any way when He ascended into heaven. We have a completely sympathetic high priest at the right hand of God!

B. Jesus is our sinless high priest.

He was "tempted in all things as we are, yet without sin." At first, we may wrongly think that being sinless would make Jesus unsympathetic and distant from us, since we all have sinned many times. Perhaps a fellow sinner could relate more to my failures. But that is not so. Charles Spurgeon pointed out (*Metropolitan Tabernacle Pulpit* [Pilgrim Publications], 36:323, italics his),

> ... do not imagine that if the Lord Jesus had sinned he would have been any more tender toward you; for *sin is always of a hardening nature*. If the Christ of God could have sinned, he would have lost the perfection of his sympathetic nature. It needs perfectness of heart to lay self all aside, and to be touched with a feeling of the infirmities of others.

Others object that if Jesus never sinned, He must not have been tempted to the degree that we are tempted. But as many have pointed out, that is not so. The one who resists to the very end knows the power of temptation in a greater way than the one who yields to sin sooner.

When it says that Jesus was tempted in all things as we are, it doesn't mean every conceivable temptation, which would be impossible. Nor was Jesus ever tempted by indwelling sin, as we are. In this, He was like Adam and Eve before the fall. Temptation had to come to Jesus from without, not from within.

But Jesus knew every type of temptation. He knew what it is like to be hungry, thirsty, and tired. He knew the horrible agony of physical torture, which He endured in His trial and crucifixion. He knew what it is like to be mocked, distrusted, maligned, and betrayed by friends. From the start of Jesus' ministry to the very end, Satan leveled all of his evil power and strategies to try to get Jesus to sin. But he never succeeded. Jesus always obeyed the Father.

Verse 15 raises the question, "Was it *possible* for Jesus to have sinned?" We need to answer this carefully (I am following Wayne Grudem, *Systematic Theology* [Zondervan], pp. 537-539). Scripture clearly affirms that Jesus never committed sin (Heb. 7:26; 1 Pet. 1:19; 2:22). It also affirms that His temptations were real, not just playacting. The Bible also affirms (James 1:13), "God cannot be tempted by evil." Since Jesus was fully God, how then could He *really* be tempted, much less commit a sin? Here we plunge into the mystery of how one man can be both fully God and fully human, as Scripture plainly affirms of Jesus.

Since Jesus is one *person* with two natures, and since sin involves the whole person, in this sense, Jesus *could not* have sinned, or He would have ceased to be God. But the question remains, "How then could Jesus' temptations be real?" The answer seems to be that Jesus met every temptation to sin, not by His divine power, but by His human nature relying on the power of the Father and Holy Spirit. As Wayne Grudem explains (p. 539), "The moral strength of his divine nature was there as a sort of 'backstop' that would have prevented him from sinning..., but he did not rely on the strength of his divine nature to make it easier for him to face temptations...."

As you know, Scripture sometimes affirms something of Jesus that could only be true of one of His natures, but not both (Matt. 24:36). Jesus' divine nature could not be tempted or sin, but His human nature could. Don't stumble over the fact that you cannot fully comprehend this. Rather, accept the testimony of Scripture: Jesus truly was tempted, and He never sinned. These facts mean that He understands what we are going through, and He is able to come to our aid when we are tempted (2:18).

Because Jesus is a sympathetic and sinless high priest…

C. We should draw near in prayer.

"Draw near with confidence to the throne of grace, so that we may receive mercy and find grace to help in time of need." "Throne of grace" is an oxymoron. To the ancient world, a throne was a forbidding place of sovereign authority and judgment. If you approached a throne and the king did not hold out his scepter, you were history! You definitely would not draw near to the throne for sympathy, especially with a trivial problem. But the author calls it the throne *of grace*. He makes it clear that we are *welcome* at this throne. He answers four questions: (1) *Why* draw near? (2) *When* should we draw near? (3) *How* should we draw near? And, (4) *What* can we expect when we draw near?

> 1) *Why* draw near? We should draw near to the throne of grace because we are weak and we have there a sympathetic high priest.

We don't come because we've got it pretty much together and we just need a little advice. We come because we are weak (4:15). Jesus didn't say, "Without Me, you can get along pretty well most of the time. Call Me if you need Me." He said (John 15:5), "Without Me, you can do nothing." And when we come to the throne of grace, He doesn't ridicule us or belittle us for our weaknesses. He welcomes us as a father welcomes his children to his side to protect them from some danger.

> 2) *When* should we draw near? We should draw near to the throne of grace whenever we need help.

We should come in a "time of need," which is at *all* times! A main reason we do not pray is that we don't realize how needy we are. We think we can handle things on our own. Just call in the Lord when things get really intense. But the fact is, we depend on Him for every breath we take and for every meal we eat, even if we've got a month's supply of food in the freezer. Praying without ceasing (1 Thess. 5:17) is necessary because we are constantly in over our heads. Prayer is the acknowledgement that our need is not partial; it is *total!*

The Throne of Grace

3) *How* should we draw near? We should draw near to the throne of grace directly, with confidence in our high priest.

The author does not say, "Draw near through your local priest." He says, "Let *us* draw near." *Us* means every believer. Dr. Dwight Pentecost, one of my professors in seminary, told how he was in Mexico City during a feast for the Immaculate Conception of Mary. There was a long line of thousands waiting for confession, but only one confession booth. As the noon bells rang, an old, stooped over priest came out of the booth, walking with two canes. A woman with several small children fell on her knees before him and grabbed him by the knees. She cried out to him, begging him to relieve her burdens. But he struck her on the side of the head with one of his canes and went off through the crowd. He was an unsympathetic, weak human priest.

Thankfully, we do not have to go through any human priest to draw near to the very throne of God. We could not dare come in our own merit or righteousness. But we can come *with confidence* because the blood of Jesus, our high priest, has gained us access (Eph. 3:12). Our confidence is not in how good we've been or in how well we can pray. Spurgeon pointed out that God will overlook our shortcomings and poor prayers just as a loving parent will overlook the mistakes in the sentences of his toddler. Even when we have sinned badly, if we draw near to confess our sins, He will cleanse our wounds and begin the healing process, just as a parent would carefully clean and bandage the wounds of his child. Finally,

4) *What* can we expect when we draw near? We will receive mercy and find grace to help in our time of need.

What a wonderful promise! We won't be scolded for having a need. We won't be told that our need is too trivial for such an important high priest to be troubled with. We will receive mercy and find grace to help. "Help" is a technical nautical term that is used elsewhere only in Acts 27:17 to describe the cables that the sailors wrapped around the hull of Paul's ship during the storm so that it would not break apart. We encountered the verb in Hebrews 2:18, where it has the nuance of running to the aid of someone crying for help. When your life seems to be coming apart at the seams because of the storm, cry out to our sympathetic high priest at the throne of grace. You will receive mercy and find grace to help.

What is the difference between *mercy* and *grace?* They somewhat overlap, but *mercy* has special reference to God's tenderness toward us because of the misery caused by our sins, whereas *grace* refers to His undeserved favor in freely forgiving our sins, which actually deserve His judgment (R. C. Trench, *Synonyms of the New Testament* [Eerdmans], pp. 169-170). Together, both words reflect the good news that "God was in Christ reconciling the world to Himself, not counting their trespasses against them" (2 Cor. 5:18). All who trust in Christ and His shed blood as the payment for their sins have free access at the throne of grace to God's boundless mercy and abundant grace!

Conclusion

I like John Piper's analogy that prayer is our walkie-talkie to get the supplies we need in the spiritual war that we are engaged in. It's not an intercom to call the maid to bring extra beverages to the den. In other words, prayer isn't to make us comfortable and cozy, oblivious to the advancement of God's kingdom purposes. Prayer is our walkie-talkie to bring in the needed supplies as we seek first His kingdom and righteousness. If you're under fire in the battle, persevere—hold fast your confession, because Jesus is our great high priest. If you have needs, pray—draw near to the throne of grace to receive mercy and find grace to help in the battle.

Application Questions

1. How does our understanding of the person and work of Christ relate to persevering in trials?

2. Does Jesus' sympathy for our weaknesses mean that He tolerates our sins? Explain.

3. Some Christians argue that if Jesus could not have sinned, His temptations were not real. Is this so? Why/why not?

4. The term "throne of grace" reflects a fine balance between the reverent fear of God and being accepted by Him. Discuss the implications of this balance.

Printed in Great Britain
by Amazon